IMPACTFUL ESTATE PLANNING

How Family Dynamics, Goals, and Wishes Influence Leaving Your Inheritance and Legacy

R. SAM PRICE

PROBATEDOCS LLC
UNITED STATES OF AMERICA

Published by ProbateDocs LLC.

www.probatedocs.com

Printed in the United States of America.

ProbateDocs LLC

454 Cajon Street

Redlands, CA 92373

hello@probatedocs.com

DEDICATION

To my loving family,
May my enduring legacy be as a great husband and a great dad.

TESTIMONIALS

"Great experience. Sam is knowledgeable and friendly. He listens to our needs and gives great advice. The office staff is very helpful and efficient as well. Highly recommend!."

– Y. Zhang

*

"The team at Price Law Firm was awesome! They helped me out with the administration of a family member's trust. Without them, I would have been dead in the water, not knowing where or how to begin. Their price was reasonable for the peace of mind and time that they saved my family and I. I highly recommend the Price Law Firm to anyone that needs assistance managing a trust."

– A. Gomber

*

"Had a great experience doing my estate planning here. John and Mia were very helpful answering all my questions & communicated well throughout the whole process. Walked in there not knowing anything & definitely got the help I needed. They Finished up in a timely manner & feel so much better having these documents that share my decisions & protect me. Highly recommend."

– R. Carreon

*

"Sam Price was very professional. He took the time to understand our needs and tailored a plan to meet those needs."

– N. Sundstrom

*

"Sam is a superior attorney. He is so smart, and he listens. He gave us expert legal advice, and his team is personable. He answered all of our questions and worked on everything expeditiously. We never felt like we were not as important as any other of his clients. We will go to him again whenever we need help."

– Rebecca

"This law firm was so efficient and provided fabulous customer service. I am so pleased with all that the staff did in every detail. I highly recommend Sam and his expertise The staff is fantastic and so understanding. It's so difficult these days to find good customer service but not at this firm. Too bad there are not enough stars to rate this company higher."

– Christine F.

*

"Polite staff, kept appointment on time, went through the process, Sam took the time to answer all of our questions, he was professional and personable. I highly recommend Price Law Firm."

– Denise C.

*

"You've heard about the shyster, bottom-feeding lawyers? These ain't them. Sam Price is a really nice guy. The people working with him are, too. They "re-stated" (and vastly improved) my existing Revocable Trust and "forced" this old Country Girl to understand every step they took. Sam revealed potential snags I would never have thought of. The "price" for this knowledge and experience isn't an issue because Estate Planning, Trusts and all that stuff is What They DO! Find them at pricelawfirm.com, on Face Book or call (909) 475-8800. If you have any desire to settle your mind about "who gets what" after you're gone, or just want to spit in the government's face by avoiding probate or, like me, simply need to revise your existing trust, show up at one of their seminars. Even if you don't use them, you'll be smarter when you leave."

– Faye P.

*

"I did some research and read reviews, and this is why we decided to make our family trust with John and Mia at Price Law Firm. I had no idea estate planning could go horribly without an attorney. I figured that making a will and power of attorney with free forms from legal zoom would suffice until my mom's health began to decline. That was when I found articles and videos about families spending thousands and destroying relationships because they assumed, like me, that as long as we filled in the blanks, we would avoid probate. John was knowledgeable and helped us make our family trust answering every question we had. I would recommend anyone planning their estate to go with Price Law. The cost was much less than I had expected and well worth the peace of mind."

– D .Skelton

"My wife and I came in for an estate plan and I couldn't be happier with the service. Sam was very knowledgeable and took the time to explain everything. Then I came back for my business. He formed an LLC to protect my family. I would come back again for any legal services."

– Andrew D.

*

"I wanted to thank this firm for the excellent job they did on my estate plan. My wife and I needed to redo our will and trust estate plan as it was about 10 years old. Service was exceptional, the firm was responsive to all my inquiries on a complex estate plan and I met several times with attorney Sam Price. I was impressed with his knowledge and expertise in this field of law. I would highly recommend this firm for your estate plan, will and trust needs."

– C. Cleveland

*

"Mr. Price was recommended to my family by a friend, his team has done a tremendous service that my family needed. The legal knowledge and professional system they used to solve our problem was outstanding."

– J. Van Overeem

These testimonials or endorsements do not constitute a guarantee, warranty, or prediction regarding the outcome of your legal matter.

TABLE OF CONTENTS

PREFACE: ABOUT THE AUTHOR
R. SAM PRICE

About the Author: R. Sam Price, J.D., LL.M.

R. Sam Price is not merely an attorney but a guide through the complexities of estate planning, trust, and probate law. With a unique ability to demystify legal jargon and simplify intricate procedures, Sam serves as a trusted navigator for those embarking on the journey of securing their familial and financial futures.

Expertise and Recognition

As a Certified Specialist in Estate Planning, Trust, and Probate Law by The State Bar of California Board of Legal Specialization, Sam is the driving force behind Price Law Firm APC. He leads a dynamic team committed to providing exceptional legal services in estate planning, trust administration, and probate. His leadership extends to chairing the San Bernardino County Bar Association Estate Planning and Probate Section, where he organizes educational initiatives and spearheads the annual Probate Symposium. His contributions to the California Lawyers Association's Estates and Trusts Section are invaluable, particularly in legislative review.

Educational Foundation

Sam's journey in law began with a Bachelor's degree in Business Administration from California State University, San Bernardino. He earned his Juris Doctor with cum laude honors from Western New England College School of Law and continued his specialized education with a Master of Laws in Taxation from New York University School of Law. This advanced training has made him a recognized authority in estate and tax planning.

A Personal Commitment to Estate Planning

Sam's commitment to estate planning is deeply personal and stems from his own family experiences. Growing up in a family unprepared for the incapacitation and loss of his father, Sam faced firsthand the challenges and hardships that arise when proper planning is absent. This profound personal impact inspired him to specialize in estate planning to ensure that no other family would have to endure similar struggles. His passion is fueled by a desire to help others avoid the emotional and financial turmoil that his family had to confront.

Impact and Influence

Sam's prowess in estate planning and probate matters has profoundly impacted his clients and colleagues alike. An author client even featured him as a character in her novel "Battle of the Wills," a testament to his dedication and influence in the field.

A Personal Touch

Beyond his professional endeavors, Sam is a dedicated family man, cherishing time with his wife, a British TV reporter, Tiffany and their son, Parker. His personal interests include culinary arts, where he explores new recipes, and spending quality time with his family.

Through his professional expertise, educational initiatives, and personal experiences, R. Sam Price stands as a pillar of support and guidance in estate planning and probate law, committed to the well-being of his clients and their families.

A Deeper Understanding of What Families Go Through

R. Sam Price chose estate planning as his specialty because of deeply personal reasons rooted in his family history and the hardships they faced. Growing up, Sam witnessed firsthand the consequences of not having an estate plan in place when his father, fell gravely ill and was hospitalized in the intensive care unit for an extended period. During this time, his family struggled not only with the emotional toll of his father's illness but also with the practical realities of incapacity. His family was completely unprepared for the possibility that his father would become incapacitated. He wasn't able to work, handle his finances, or make medical decisions for his health care; he was heavily medicated and bedridden with tubes up his nose and down his throat.

Sam's father was only fifty-six when he passed away in the intensive care unit, at the Veteran's Administration Hospital in Long Beach, California; leaving his mother to navigate the complexities of estate settlement while raising two young children alone. Not only was his mother unprepared to cope with her husband's sudden death, she didn't know what to do or who to turn to for help. Now, a single mother of two, it was extremely challenging to manage work, and handle the confusing, long, expensive process of settling her late husband's affairs.

This formative experience instilled in Sam a profound understanding of the challenges families face during such critical times. It propelled him to pursue a career where he could apply his legal expertise to help others avoid the difficulties his family endured. Sam approaches estate planning from a place of empathy and compassion, emphasizing the importance of being prepared for life's uncertainties. His practice is not just about crafting legal documents; it's about offering guidance and support to families navigating the emotional and financial complexities of planning for the future.

Through his work, Sam aims to provide peace of mind to his clients by ensuring their wishes are honored and their families are cared for, echoing his commitment to help others achieve the security that his family lacked during their time of need.

CHAPTER 1
WHO IS THIS BOOK FOR?

Who Is This Book For?

This book is crafted for individuals and families who recognize the importance of preparing for the future but may feel overwhelmed by the legal complexities of estate planning. It is for middle-class families who want to ensure that their hard-earned assets and life's work are preserved and passed on according to their wishes. It is for the family that understands that investing some time and money in estate planning now will save a lot more time and money later. Whether you are starting a family, navigating the prime of your life, or considering retirement, this guide aims to equip you with the knowledge to make informed decisions about your estate.

There are many myths and misconceptions about estate planning, and the internet often provides conflicting advice. This book aims to clear up confusion and provide reliable information tailored to California law, helping you make the right decisions for your unique situation.

Understanding Estate Planning

Most people know that an estate plan can specify who receives their inheritance and can help avoid probate court. However, many misunderstand that all trusts are the same. In reality, each trust is unique because every family situation is different, with distinct dynamics, goals, and needs. Estate planning is about much more than just avoiding probate—it's about creating a personalized plan to solve problems and provide protections and benefits for you and your loved ones.

Creating an estate plan can be compared to getting an eye exam. Just as a prescription for glasses must fit your specific vision needs, an estate plan must fit your family's dynamics, goals, and wishes. An estate planning attorney will guide you through options, helping you decide what fits your needs from your family's point of view. Once those decisions are made, the estate plan is drafted to reflect your choices—customized to your goals and wishes.

For the Family Planner

If you are someone who takes pride in ensuring your family is well taken care of, this book is for you. Estate planning is not just about avoiding probate; it's about securing your family's financial future and making sure that your dependents are provided for in your absence. This book will help you understand how to use tools like Wills, Trusts, Powers of Attorney, and other estate planning documents to protect your loved ones, including minor children or dependents with special needs.

For the Procrastinator

Many people delay creating an estate plan because they think they have plenty of time or because it's difficult to face their own mortality. However, life is unpredictable, and having an estate plan in place is crucial for protecting your loved ones and making sure your wishes are respected. This book aims to make the estate planning process less daunting, providing the information you need to take action now rather than later.

For the Smart Investor

If you live by the idea that "a penny saved is a penny earned," than you're a smart investor. Investing the time and money now in creating an estate plan will pay off by saving a lot of time and money in the future. You save money by planning now because an estate plan is a fraction of the cost of a conservatorship or probate case. And your estate plan will save time because it is much more efficient way of distributing your wealth than a probate case that has to wind its way through the courts. Whether you want to save time, money, or both, creating your estate plan is a good investment.

For the Business Owner

If you own a business, estate planning involves an additional layer of complexity. You need to consider not only your personal assets but also the future of your business. This book provides insight into handling business succession, balancing business and personal interests, and ensuring that your legacy continues as you envision. Whether you own a family business or are a partner in a larger enterprise, integrating your business into your estate plan is crucial for long-term success.

For the Philanthropically Inclined

If giving back to your community is important to you, this book will show you how to incorporate charitable giving into your estate plan. From donor-advised funds and charitable trusts to bequests, there are many options to explore. Estate planning can help you leave a meaningful legacy that extends beyond your family and benefits the causes you care about.

Conclusion

This book is for anyone who wishes to understand the nuances of estate planning without getting lost in legal jargon. It is for those who want to make educated, thoughtful decisions about the future of their assets and their family's well-being. With a focus on clarity, compassion, and practicality, this guide aims to empower you to create a comprehensive plan that reflects your values, meets your family's unique needs, and ensures that your legacy is honored.

Estate planning is not just for the wealthy—it is for anyone who owns a home or has loved ones they want to protect. Many of my clients are middle-class families who have been thinking about getting their affairs in order for years. Often, it takes a significant life event, like a death in the family, a surgery, or an overseas trip, to prompt them to take action. This book is here to help you start planning before the unexpected happens.

CHAPTER 2

WHAT IS ESTATE PLANNING, AND WHY DOES IT MATTER?

What is Estate Planning About?

Many people think that estate planning is simply about deciding who gets their assets when they pass away. However, estate planning involves much more than that. It's about creating a plan that ensures someone you trust has the authority to act for you in an emergency, without needing court involvement. An estate plan helps you avoid conservatorship if you become incapacitated and probate after you pass away. But beyond that, a good estate plan deals with your unique family dynamics and complies with your goals and wishes. In the end, an estate plan is a comprehensive roadmap that provides peace of mind.

Estate planning is about protecting yourself and your loved ones during times of crisis. It helps ensure that your property is managed for your benefit while you are alive, that you and your loved ones are cared for if you become incapacitated, and that your assets are distributed according to your wishes after your death. Additionally, estate planning can help you save on taxes, professional fees, and court costs.

We design estate plans by considering your hierarchy of needs: first, taking care of you and your spouse; second, providing for your family members; third, preserving your wealth; and lastly, reducing taxes and avoiding probate.

Creating an estate must fit your family's dynamics, goals, and wishes. An estate planning attorney will guide you through options, helping you decide what fits your needs from your family's point of view. Once those decisions are made, the estate plan is drafted to reflect your choices—customized to your goals and wishes.

The Importance of Estate Planning

1. Protecting Loved Ones: The primary reason most people engage in estate planning is to ensure their loved ones are provided for in the best possible manner. This includes appointing guardians for minor children, setting up trusts to manage the family's financial needs, and ensuring a surviving spouse is supported.
2. Investing Time and Money Now Saves Time and Money Later: An investment of your time and money now in your estate plan will greatly save the time and money needed later to deal with your possible incapacity or your eventual death. Planning ahead helps avoid complications and costs that can arise without a clear plan in place.
3. Avoiding Probate: Many estate plans are set up with the goal of avoiding probate. Probate can be a public, lengthy, and costly process that can diminish the estate's value and delay the distribution of assets to beneficiaries.
4. Preparing for Incapacity: Estate planning is not just about planning for death; it's also about making arrangements for the possibility of becoming incapacitated. By establishing powers of attorney and healthcare directives, individuals can

dictate their wishes regarding their healthcare and financial affairs if they are unable to manage them themselves.

5. Planning for Property Taxes: Many people own their homes with a very low property tax base because they purchased them years ago. If the goal is to pass the family home to a child or grandchild, careful planning can help maintain that low property tax base, despite recent changes in the law that make it harder to do so.
6. Reducing Capital Gains for Married Couples: Many married couples hold title to their home as "husband and wife as joint tenants." This common mistake can lead to significant capital gains taxes for the surviving spouse. Fixing the title to ensure it qualifies as community property can help the surviving spouse benefit from a full step-up in basis, reducing potential tax liabilities.
7. Asset Protection for Your Primary Residence: California law provides some protection for your primary residence through an automatic homestead exemption, but this protection is limited. To maximize protection—up to $600,000 of equity—you need to file a homestead declaration, which extends the exemption to voluntary sales of your home.
8. Reducing Estate Taxes: Although not a concern for the vast majority of families, proper estate planning can help protect the estate from significant taxation, ensuring that more of the assets pass to the heirs.

Why Do We Need An Estate Plan?

You want to know that you are in control and that in a time of need the decisions will be yours and not someone else's. Everyone has an estate plan whether they know it or not... written in the Probate Code by the State of California. These are the default rules the come into play if you do not plan ahead of time and put that plan into action.

What happens if you're alive, but cannot make your own decisions? Without an estate plan in place, if you become incapacitated you will require a court proceeding called a conservatorship for the court to put someone in charge to make financial and medical decisions for you.

A conservatorship is an intrusive, public, burdensome and expensive court process that appoints someone to act for you if you are alive but cannot make decisions for yourself because you are incapacitated. If you don't plan ahead, then you won't be able to choose ahead of time who will take care of you or be able to leave any written instructions of what you want to have done.

What happens when you die? Without an estate plan in place, the California laws of intestate succession determine who will get your assets at your passing and you'll have to go through a time-consuming and expensive probate court proceeding to be able to pay your bills and transfer the remaining assets to your heirs. Creating an estate plan puts you in control and implements what you want, instead of the default plan that California has already written for you.

Generally, California intestate succession laws provide that all community property go to your surviving spouse and any separate property goes one-half or one-third to your surviving spouse, depending on what other heirs you leave. Your children will inherit your assets equally, and if any child pre-deceases you then his or her share will be given to his or her children (your grandchildren). However, stepchildren and foster children do not inherit under the California intestate succession laws. So, if you pass away and your spouse inherits everything, if your spouse is not the parent of your children, then they may not get their inheritance.

Even if you want the default the same distribution as the California intestate succession laws, you still need an estate plan to avoid probate.

Why Estate Planning Matters

Estate planning is crucial because it gives you control over how your assets will be handled after your death or if you become incapacitated. Your estate plan can either affirm that your goals and wishes are to have the default distribution under intestate succession, or you can change the distribution of your assets from the default rules. It helps protect your heirs from a significant tax burden and ensures that your wishes are followed, reducing disputes among surviving relatives. It's not just for the wealthy; everyone can benefit from having a clear estate plan.

Conclusion

Understanding estate planning is essential for everyone. Whether it's providing for your family after you're gone or ensuring your wishes are respected in the event of incapacity, a well-structured estate plan is invaluable. This chapter has laid the foundation for the following chapters, which will delve deeper into each component of estate planning, ensuring you are well-equipped to create a plan that fits your unique needs and provides peace of mind.

CHAPTER 3

WHAT IS PROBATE AND CONSERVATORSHIP WHY SHOULD THEY BE AVOIDED?

What Is a Probate Court Proceeding and Why Should I Avoid It?

Probate is a court-supervised process that gathers your assets, pays your debts, and distributes the remaining assets to your heirs. It is overseen by a judge and involves filing documents with the court and notifying relevant parties.

Why Probate Costs a Lot of Money

Probate can be a very expensive process. The attorney handling the probate case, as well as the executor managing the estate, are both entitled to statutory fees based on a percentage of the estate's value. These fees are calculated on the gross fair market value of the estate without deducting mortgages or other debts. The following percentages apply:

- 4% of the first $100,000
- 3% of the next $100,000
- 2% of the next $800,000
- 1% of the next $9,000,000
- 0.5% of the next $15,000,000
- Over $25,000,000, a reasonable fee

Calculation of the Statutory Fee for Ordinary Services
for Each of the Personal Representative and Attorney

Fee Basis for calculation of ordinary fees

The basis upon which the ordinary fees are calculated start with the inventory and appraisal, plus receipts, plus gains on sales, plus net income from a business, less losses on sales, less losses from a business, as follows:

Inventory and Appraisal Value
+ Receipts
+ Gains on Sales
+ Net Income From Business
- Losses on Sales
- Net Loss from Business
= Fee Base

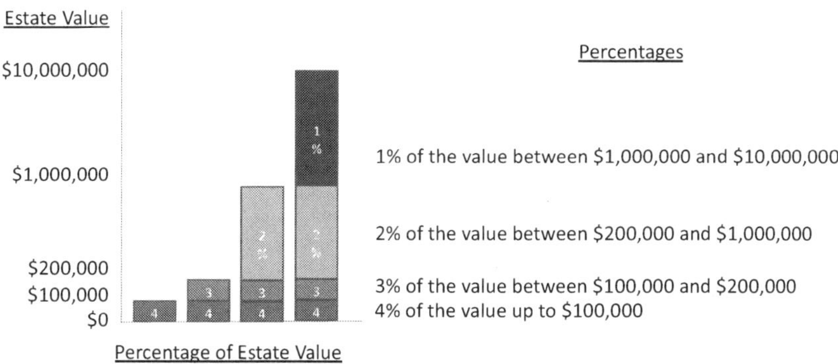

Each of the attorney and the personal representative are entitled to a fee for the ordinary services of a probate case set by California law as a percentage of the total gross value (not reduced by mortgages) of all assets of the estate according to their appraised value, plus receipts, plus gains on sale, less losses on sales.

For example, for a total value of $500,000, the statutory fee would be:

$ 4,000 (4% of the first $100,000)
+ $ 3,000 (3% of the next $100,000)
+ $ 6,000 (2% of the next $300,000)
$13,000 total

For example, if the gross value of an estate is $500,000, the statutory fees for ordinary services would be calculated as follows:

$4,000 (4% of the first $100,000)
+ $3,000 (3% of the next $100,000)
+ $6,000 (2% of the next $300,000)
= $13,000 (total ordinary fees)

The total ordinary fees amount to $13,000, which is just for the attorney. Adding the executor's fees and other costs, the total can easily reach tens of thousands of dollars. For a $500,000 estate, the costs might look like this:

- $13,000 Probate attorney's fees
- $13,000 Executor's fees
- $2,500 Court and other costs

Total: $28,500 in fees and costs.

With the high costs of a probate case, it's clear that investing in estate planning now can save significantly in the future.

Probate Takes a Long Time

In addition to being costly, probate is also a lengthy process. Even a simple probate case without complications can take between eight to twelve months to complete. More complex cases, especially those involving disputes, creditor claims, or difficulty locating heirs, can take much longer. Delays have also become more common since the COVID-19 pandemic due to increased probate filings and court backlogs.

These delays mean that heirs may have to wait for years before receiving their inheritance.

Probate Is a Public Process

Another drawback of probate is that it is a public proceeding. This means that all of your personal information, such as the value of your assets, the identity of your heirs, and your creditors, becomes part of the public record. Anyone can access this information, which can lead to privacy concerns, unwanted solicitations, and even security risks for your heirs.

Probate Causes a Loss of Control

The biggest problem with probate is that you lose control over how your assets are distributed. A judge, who doesn't know you or your family, will determine how to pay your debts and distribute your assets according to state law. This loss of control can be avoided through proper estate planning.

Tools to Avoid Probate

Fortunately, probate can often be avoided by implementing certain estate planning tools:

- Trusts: Real estate and other assets held in the name of a trust bypass probate entirely. By transferring assets such as real estate, bank accounts, and personal property into a trust, you can ensure they are distributed according to your wishes without the need for probate.
- Beneficiary Designations: For assets that cannot be transferred to a trust, such as retirement accounts, life insurance, and annuities, you should name primary and alternate beneficiaries. By designating beneficiaries, these assets can also avoid probate.

What Is a Conservatorship Court Proceeding and Why Should I Avoid It?

A conservatorship is a court proceeding that appoints someone to act on your behalf if you become incapacitated. There are two types of conservatorships:

- Conservatorship of the Person: This allows your conservator to make medical and personal decisions for you.
- Conservatorship of the Estate: This gives your conservator control over your financial assets.

Like probate, conservatorship is an expensive and invasive process. Attorney's fees and court costs for even a simple conservatorship can reach $15,000 or more, and ongoing court filings and hearings are required. Additionally, all information in a conservatorship becomes public record, compromising your privacy.

Most importantly, a conservatorship results in a significant loss of control. A judge will make decisions about your medical care, financial matters, and even personal issues like the right to vote or decisions about marriage. This loss of autonomy is why it is so crucial to avoid a conservatorship if possible.

Summary

Probate and conservatorship are costly, lengthy, and invasive court proceedings that result in a loss of control and privacy. By proactively creating an estate plan with tools like trusts and beneficiary designations, you can avoid these processes, save money, and ensure your wishes are respected, both during your lifetime and after your death.

CHAPTER 4

WHAT DOCUMENTS ARE IN AN ESTATE PLAN?

What Are the Basic Items in an Estate Plan and What Does Each Item Typically Do?

An estate plan is all about ensuring you and your loved ones are cared for, especially during times when you might not be able to make decisions for yourself. This chapter will walk you through the different documents that make up an estate plan, why they are important, and how they help protect you and your family.

The main goal is to make sure you are taken care of during your lifetime, even if you become unable to manage your own affairs. This involves creating documents that allow someone you trust to make decisions for you if you are incapacitated. Without these documents, a court case called a conservatorship might be needed. To avoid this, an estate plan includes several key documents: a

Power of Attorney, an Advance Health Care Directive, a HIPAA Waiver, and a Nomination of Conservator.

Let's dive into each document and what it does.

Power of Attorney

A Power of Attorney is a document that allows someone you trust, called your agent, to make financial decisions on your behalf if you become unable to do so. This can include paying bills, managing your assets, or even selling your home if needed. By creating this document, you avoid the need for a conservatorship, which is a lengthy court process to appoint someone to make these decisions for you.

We typically create a "durable" Power of Attorney, which means that it remains active even if you become incapacitated. This way, your agent can step in to manage financial matters without interruption. For extra security, we can make it a "springing" Power of Attorney, which only takes effect if you become incapacitated. This gives you more control and ensures that no one else can act on your behalf unless you are truly unable to do so.

Your agent under a Power of Attorney must act in your best interest—they have a legal obligation to manage your assets responsibly. This is called a fiduciary duty, meaning they must always prioritize your needs above their own.

Advance Health Care Directive

An Advance Health Care Directive allows your chosen agent to make medical decisions for you if you cannot make them yourself. This document helps avoid the need for a conservatorship, ensuring your healthcare decisions stay in the hands of someone you trust.

If you're able to communicate your wishes, doctors will follow your instructions. But if you're incapacitated—like if you're unconscious or unable to understand what's happening—your agent can step in. Your Advance Health Care Directive can include specific instructions on the type of care you want, ensuring your preferences are respected even when you cannot express them. This way, you maintain control over your healthcare choices, even if you need someone else to speak on your behalf.

HIPAA Waiver

HIPAA laws protect your medical information, keeping it private. While this is great for privacy, it can also prevent doctors from sharing important information with your family if you're unable to give permission. That's where a HIPAA Waiver comes in.

A HIPAA Waiver allows your doctors to share your medical information with your chosen agent. This is crucial because it allows your agent to understand your medical condition and make informed decisions about your care. The HIPAA Waiver works together with your Advance Health Care Directive to make sure your agent has all the information needed to act in your best interest.

Nomination of Conservator

Although the documents we've discussed are designed to avoid the need for a conservatorship, it's always smart to have a backup plan. A Nomination of Conservator is a document that allows you to choose who you want to be appointed as your conservator if a court ever needs to step in.

This ensures that, even if the other documents somehow don't work as intended, you still have control over who takes care of you. It's about being prepared for every possibility and making sure your wishes are respected.

A Will: Its Benefits and Limitations

A Will is a legal document that lets you decide who will receive your assets when you pass away. It also allows you to appoint an executor—a person responsible for handling your assets, paying bills, and distributing your inheritance to your beneficiaries. This helps ensure that your wishes are followed after your death.

However, if you own real estate in your name, a Will alone isn't enough. In California, real estate owned in your name must go through a court process called probate, even if you have a Will. That's why we often recommend a trust-based estate plan for those who own property—to avoid the probate process entirely.

The Need for a Will Even with Other Estate Planning Tools

Even if you have other estate planning tools, such as a trust, a Will is still essential. A type of Will called a "Pour-Over Will" ensures that any assets not properly transferred into your trust are added to it after your death. This makes sure all your assets are distributed according to your wishes.

A Pour-Over Will also names an executor, which prevents family conflicts over who should manage your estate. It serves as a safety net, catching anything that wasn't placed in your trust during your lifetime.

What Is a Trust?

A Trust is another document that allows you to decide who will receive your assets, but it has the added benefit of helping you avoid probate. A Revocable Living Trust is a type of trust that can be changed or canceled during your lifetime, and it takes effect while you're still alive.

A Trust involves three roles:

- Settlor: The person who creates the Trust.

- Trustee: The person who manages the Trust's assets.
- Beneficiary: The person who benefits from the Trust's assets.

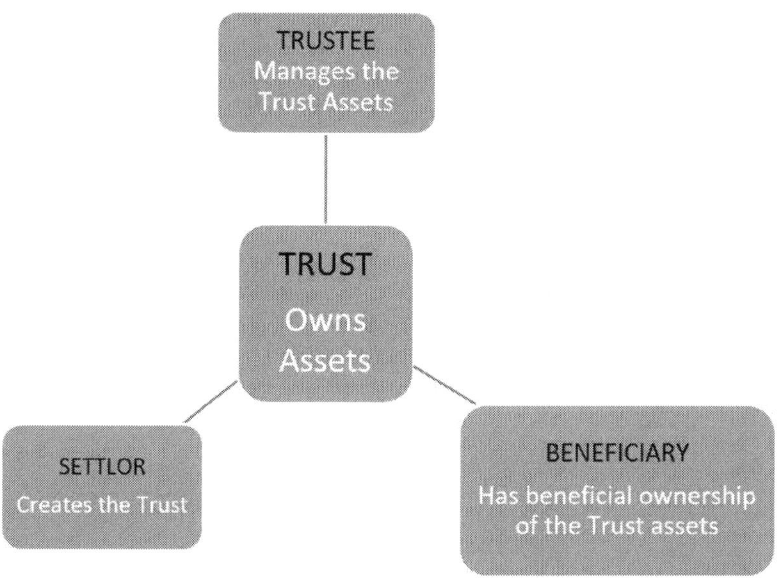

Often, you will be all three roles—you create the Trust, manage it, and benefit from it. This allows you to maintain control over your assets while making sure they are handled according to your wishes if you become incapacitated or after you pass away.

To make a Trust effective, you need to transfer your assets into it. This is called "funding" the Trust, and it's an important step that ensures your assets are covered by the terms of the Trust.

Will I Lose Control of My Assets If I Create a Trust?

Many people worry they will lose control of their assets if they create a Trust. Rest assured; you remain in control. You continue to manage your assets, make purchases, and conduct business just as you always have. The Trust simply acts as a container, holding your assets while allowing you to use them freely. The only time you lose direct control is if you become incapacitated, at which point your chosen Successor Trustee steps in to manage things for you.

Differences Between a Last Will and Testament and a Revocable Living Trust

Both a Will and a Revocable Living Trust let you determine who will receive your assets, but they have some important differences:

- Incapacity: A Will only takes effect when you die, while a Trust can take care of you if you become incapacitated. A Trust allows your Successor Trustee to manage your assets without needing a court-appointed conservator.
- Probate Avoidance: A Will requires a probate case to transfer assets, whereas a Trust avoids probate altogether, allowing for a quicker and more private transfer of assets.
- Trust Funding: A Will covers all your assets without additional steps, but a Trust requires that you transfer your assets into it—a critical step to ensure your wishes are followed.

Summary

An estate plan is about keeping you in control, even if you can't communicate your wishes or make decisions. Documents like the Power of Attorney, Advance Health Care Directive, HIPAA Waiver, and Nomination of Conservator help ensure that you are cared for during your lifetime. Tools like a Will and a Revocable Living Trust work together to make sure your assets are distributed according to your wishes without unnecessary court involvement.

With a properly prepared estate plan, you can rest assured that your loved ones will be taken care of and that your wishes will be respected—without the stress and expense of court procedures.

CHAPTER 5

WHAT IS YOUR ESTATE PLANNING PROCESS?

The Estate Planning Process

Clients often come to us after a significant life event, such as an upcoming flight, surgery, or a recent death in the family. The estate planning process ensures that all potential concerns are addressed, allowing you to feel confident that you've considered everything. By guiding you step-by-step, we make sure you have a plan that meets your needs and provides peace of mind for you and your loved ones.

Overview of Legal Ethics in Estate Planning

Before engaging an attorney for estate planning services, it's important to understand some key legal ethics.

- Duty of Confidentiality: Attorneys are bound by a strict duty of

confidentiality, which means they must keep all information shared by their clients private. This ensures that clients can speak openly without fear of disclosure. When representing a married couple, the attorney cannot keep secrets between them; anything shared by one spouse must be shared with the other. Transparency is necessary for effective representation.
- Potential Conflicts of Interest: Representing a married couple carries the potential for conflicts of interest, especially if the spouses have different goals or preferences. If an irreconcilable conflict arises, the attorney must withdraw from representing both spouses, and each spouse must obtain separate legal representation to protect their individual interests.

The Estate Planning Process: Step-by-Step

Our estate planning process has seven steps to ensure that we provide consistent, quality legal services and that all of your needs are covered.

Our Estate Planning Process

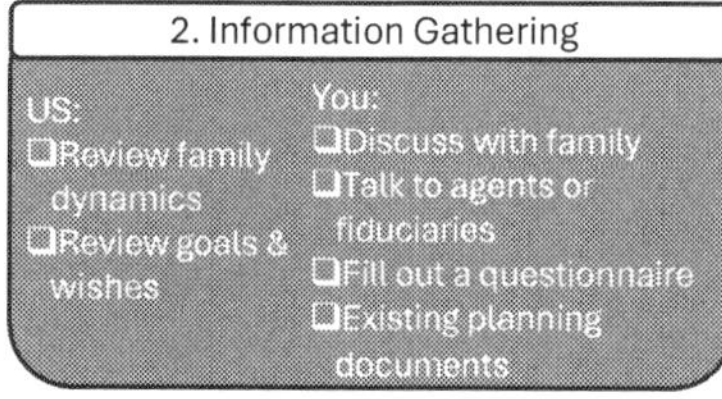

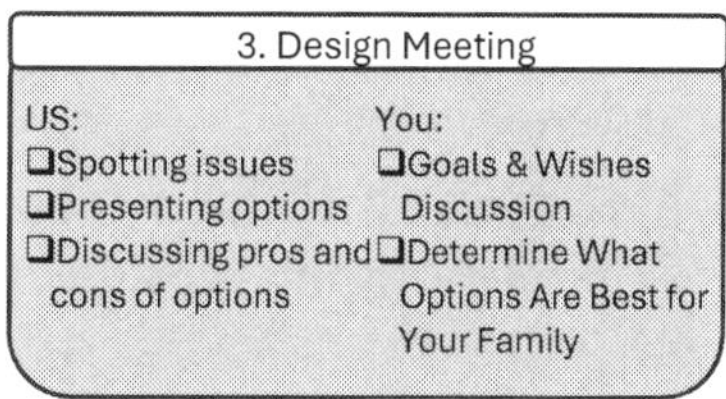

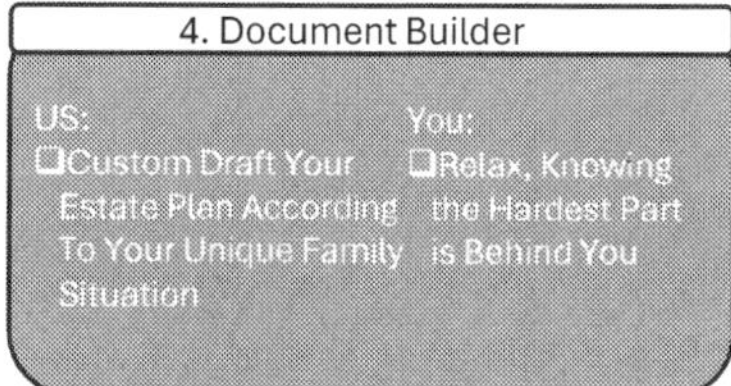

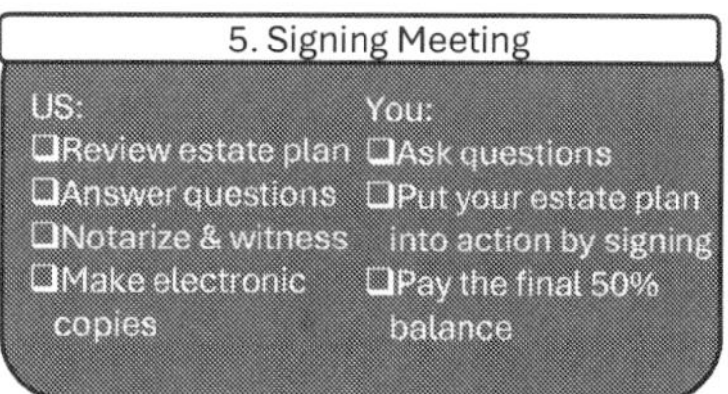

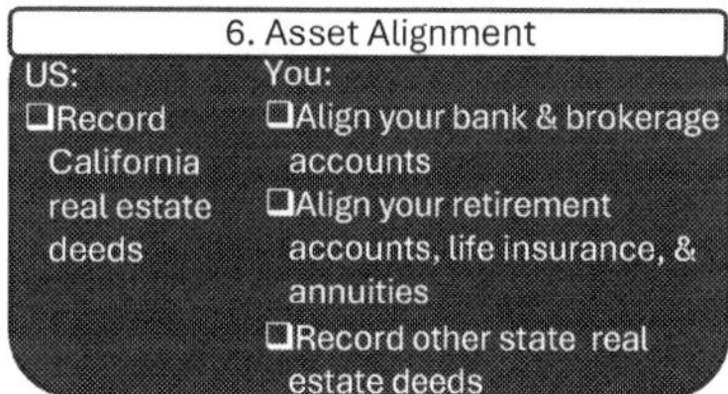

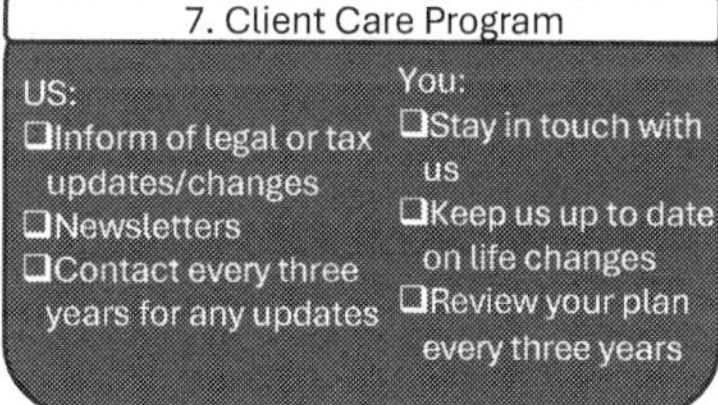

1. Right Fit Meeting: You meet with a Client Care Specialist to discuss what estate planning is about, learn about our estate planning process, and go over our plans and pricing. You then choose a plan, sign an engagement agreement, and pay a 50% deposit to set up a design meeting.
2. Information Gathering: You fill out a questionnaire so that we can gather information about your family, assets, goals, and

wishes. We review the estate planning questionnaire to gain an understanding of your unique family situation and what you want your estate plan to do for you.

3. Design Meeting: At the design meeting, we discuss your family dynamics, goals, and wishes. This can be the lengthiest part of the estate planning process and sometimes involves more than one meeting. We may bring up issues that you hadn't considered and need time to think about or discuss further with family members. Our job is to think ahead and anticipate potential issues, offering options for handling them along with the pros and cons of each choice. After understanding the issues and their impact on your family, you decide on the best options.
4. Document Builder: Once the design is finalized, we draft the estate planning documents that put your unique estate planning design into action. This involves coordinating each document to reflect your goals and wishes accurately. Your estate planning documents are placed in a heavy-duty binder for archival. Depending on the complexity of your plan, this process can take one to four weeks. In emergencies, we can sometimes accommodate a quicker timeline. We also implement a multi-point quality control system to ensure the documents are drafted correctly.
5. Signing Meeting: We review your estate plan with you and answer any questions. Using easy-to-understand language, we explain everything so that you know what your estate plan does and how it works. Our notary public and witness assist in signing the documents, putting your estate plan into action. You take your estate planning binder home and put your originals in a safe place. We also make an electronic copy to store safely in case the originals are lost or stolen. This is often when our clients feel a sense of relief, knowing their loved ones are taken care of.
6. Asset Alignment: After the signing meeting, we move on to asset alignment. Trusts require a second step after being created—funding the trust with your assets. Proper alignment ensures that your assets are available for you while you're alive or incapacitated and are distributed to your loved ones after

your passing. This involves retitling assets, such as real estate, bank accounts, and investment accounts, into the name of the trust. For example, real estate must be transferred to the trust, and financial accounts must be retitled in the name of the trustees. We coordinate these changes to ensure everything aligns with your estate plan.

7. Client Care Program: Finally, our Client Care Program ensures that your estate plan stays up to date. Many people think of their estate plan as something they can "set and forget," but changes in family dynamics, goals, assets, and the law require ongoing adjustments. Our Client Care Program allows us to keep in regular contact with you, follow up every three years to see if anything has changed, and inform you of any major legal and tax changes that may affect your plan. We also help with asset alignment for any new purchases or changes, ensuring your plan remains effective.

Summary

Our estate planning process is designed to be thorough, ensuring every aspect of your needs and concerns is addressed. By guiding you through each step, from initial consultation to keeping your plan current, we aim to provide you with peace of mind knowing that you and your loved ones are protected, no matter what the future brings.

CHAPTER 6

PLANNING FOR POSSIBLE INCAPACITY

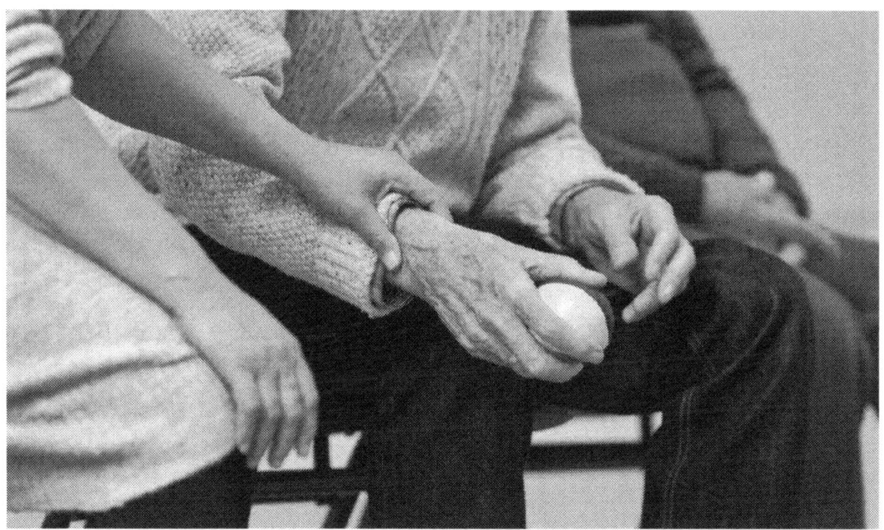

Incapacity and the Importance of Planning Ahead

Incapacity refers to a physical or mental inability to manage your own affairs. This might occur due to conditions like Alzheimer's or dementia, or because of an event like a stroke, being unconscious, in a vegetative state, or suffering from severe head trauma. Essentially, incapacity is any situation where you are unable to communicate your wishes.

While many people assume this won't happen to them, a 2017 national study by the Cornell University Institute on Employment and Disability reported that 25.1% of people aged 65 to 74 had a disability. Among those aged 75 and older, nearly half—48.7%—reported a disability. The possibility of becoming incapacitated is more common than you might think, and planning for it is a critical part of securing your future.

Imagine a loved one standing in a hospital hallway, stressed and worried, trying to make decisions for you. Without a plan in place, your loved one may not have the legal authority to make those decisions or access your medical information. This is the worst possible time to find out that the necessary legal documents aren't available, leaving your loved one overwhelmed, unsure of your wishes, and unable to act. This is why having a written plan specifying who will take over if you are incapacitated and what guidelines they should follow is so important.

The Importance of a Financial Power of Attorney

A financial power of attorney allows your chosen agent to manage your finances if you become incapacitated. This includes collecting income, paying bills, and handling any other financial matters. Without a power of attorney in place, your family may need to go through an expensive and time-consuming court process to obtain the authority to manage your finances.

The Problem with the Statutory Form Power of Attorney

The California statutory form power of attorney has several limitations:

- General vs. Durable Power of Attorney: The statutory form is a general power of attorney that terminates if you become incapacitated. This is the opposite of what you need! Instead, you need a durable power of attorney that remains active even after you are incapacitated, allowing your agent to continue managing your affairs.
- Springing vs. Immediate Power of Attorney: By default, the statutory form is an immediate power of attorney, meaning it becomes active as soon as you sign it. This can expose your assets to misuse if the agent is not trustworthy. A better option is a springing power of attorney, which only becomes active

once a doctor determines you are unable to handle your own finances.

- Additional Powers: The statutory form includes certain basic powers, but many financial institutions require specific language authorizing certain actions. For example, without a specific provision about dealing with annuities or accessing a safe deposit box, your agent may not be able to manage these assets effectively. The statutory form is often insufficient to grant all the necessary powers to your agent.

How We Improve the Statutory Form Power of Attorney

At Price Law Firm, APC, we customize a durable power of attorney to ensure your agent can properly manage your financial affairs. We include 26 additional special powers that cover a wide range of potential situations, based on our experience dealing with financial institutions. For instance, we include specific language about accessing safe deposit boxes, which is often missing from the standard form.

By making these improvements, we ensure that your agent will have the authority to manage your finances effectively, whether that involves paying bills, selling assets, or handling other financial matters. We also make our durable power of attorney a "springing" power of attorney, meaning it only takes effect if you become incapacitated.

The Importance of an Advanced Healthcare Directive

An advanced healthcare directive is another essential part of an estate plan. This document gives your chosen agent the authority to make medical decisions on your behalf if you are unable to do so. It allows you to provide specific instructions regarding your healthcare, including your preferences for end-of-life care, and ensures your wishes are respected.

You can be as detailed as you like, specifying particular treatments you do or do not want. Alternatively, you can leave some decisions to your agent's discretion, based on the medical information they receive. Your agent also has the authority to make decisions regarding the disposition of your remains, whether by burial or cremation, according to your wishes.

The Role of a HIPAA Waiver

The Health Insurance Portability and Accountability Act (HIPAA) is a federal law that protects your confidential medical information. While this privacy protection is essential, it can create barriers when your agent needs to access your medical information to make informed decisions on your behalf. A HIPAA waiver allows your agent to receive your confidential medical information, ensuring they can effectively carry out their duties under the advanced healthcare directive.

Summary

Planning for incapacity is an essential part of estate planning. A durable power of attorney, an advanced healthcare directive, and a HIPAA waiver all work together to ensure that if you become incapacitated, the right person has the authority to manage your finances and make medical decisions for you. By putting these documents in place, you can avoid the stress and expense of a conservatorship, protect your privacy, and ensure your wishes are followed.

CHAPTER 7
PLANNING TO ACHIEVE THE GOALS AND WISHES OF A FAMILY

The Typical Estate Planning Client's Goals

Most clients who come to us for estate planning want to ensure that they are well taken care of during their lifetime, especially if they become incapacitated. They also want to protect and safeguard the assets they have spent their lives accumulating. If one spouse passes away, the primary goal is to ensure that the surviving spouse is well cared for. After both spouses are gone, the focus shifts to taking care of their family, which may include children, grandchildren, parents, nieces, nephews, or even close friends who are like family. Ultimately, the goal is to make sure that your loved ones are taken care of after your passing.

Goals of an Estate Plan

A well-designed estate plan allows individuals to care for themselves and their loved ones, ensuring that their wealth is preserved, and avoiding unnecessary taxes, conservatorships, and probate. It also ensures a smooth transition for both you and your family if you become disabled or pass away.

One of the lesser-known goals of estate planning is to maintain harmony and preserve peace within the family after your death. Money can bring out unresolved family tensions, and old feuds may resurface during stressful times. An estate plan can be designed to minimize the potential for disputes and keep the family relationships intact.

No one wants their hard-earned money to end up in the wrong hands—whether that means taxes, probate court costs, an ex-son-in-law, or a child's creditors. A properly designed estate plan can ensure that these unwanted parties are kept away from your inheritance.

Major Considerations in Planning an Estate

There are three major considerations that we take into account when planning an estate:

1. *Family Dynamics*

Every family is unique, and we need to plan around each client's specific circumstances. We strive to ensure that the estate plan accounts for the dynamics within your family. In later chapters, we discuss different family situations, the issues that may arise, and the options available to address them. It is ultimately up to you to decide what is best for you and your family.

2. *Asset Mix*

Each family has a different asset mix, which requires specific planning for each type of asset. For a married couple, assets may include both separate and community property. The couple may wish to treat all assets as community property or distribute certain assets differently among beneficiaries.

For real estate, it is essential that all properties, such as a home, rental property, or land, are titled in the name of the Trustees of the Revocable Living Trust. The Successor Trustee must be able to maintain the property, which may include paying the mortgage, taxes, insurance, and maintenance costs. Real estate is often sold to cover expenses and provide beneficiaries with a cash inheritance.

Financial accounts, such as checking and savings accounts, certificates of deposit, investments, and money market accounts, should also be retitled in the name of the Trustees of the Revocable Living Trust. This provides the Successor Trustee with a readily available source of cash to cover expenses. Although it is possible to name a beneficiary for financial accounts, this is not advisable since it does not protect you during your lifetime and may require probate if the beneficiary predeceases you. The best practice is to place financial accounts in the Revocable Living Trust.

Tangible personal property, including items like firearms, jewelry, art, coin collections, furniture, and antiques, should also be transferred to the Revocable Living Trust. Because these items do not have a title document, they can be transferred by signing an affidavit declaring that all tangible personal property is part of the trust. We also create a memorandum that allows you to designate specific gifts of personal property to individuals without needing to update the entire estate plan.

Vehicles, trailers, recreational vehicles, and boats are generally not transferred to the Revocable Living Trust. The California Vehicle Code allows for easy transfer of these assets without requiring probate.

Businesses also need to be addressed in an estate plan. A business could be structured as a sole proprietorship, partnership, limited partnership, LLC, or corporation. Any business interests must be transferred to the trust, and it's important to plan for who will take over the business or wind it down.

Retirement accounts, such as IRAs, require special planning to account for IRS rules. A spouse who inherits an IRA has more flexibility, while other beneficiaries must withdraw the entire balance within ten years. Naming an IRA Trust as the beneficiary of a retirement account can provide added control and creditor protection for the inherited funds.

3. *Goals and Wishes*

Every family has unique goals and wishes. This is about what you want your estate plan to do for you and your family. These may include avoiding probate and estate taxes, ensuring you are taken care of if you become incapacitated, and protecting your loved one's inheritance from spouses, lawsuits, or creditors. You may want to ensure that your beneficiaries receive a good education or that their inheritance is used wisely.

Some parents wish to distribute their estate unevenly between children due to differing financial circumstances, special needs, or personal preferences. Others want to encourage beneficiaries to pursue higher education or other opportunities.

Maintaining harmony within the family is also an important goal. Choosing a Successor Trustee who will be perceived as fair and equitable can help prevent conflicts among beneficiaries. Additionally, holding funds in a trust until all children reach a certain age can help ensure that younger children receive the same support as their older siblings.

There are many goals and wishes that are unique to each family. An estate plan can address these goals and help you achieve more than you might expect.

Summary

An estate plan is about more than just distributing assets after your death. It's about ensuring your own care during your lifetime, protecting your loved ones, and achieving your personal goals. By taking into account family dynamics, asset mix, and your specific wishes, we can create an estate plan that addresses all of your needs and ensures a smooth and peaceful transition for your family.

CHAPTER 8

HOW FAMILY DYNAMICS AFFECT ESTATE PLANNING

When embarking on estate planning, one critical aspect often overlooked is the impact of family dynamics. Understanding and considering the relationships within your family are vital as they significantly influence how you should approach the planning process. Every family is unique, with its own set of relationships, challenges, and interactions that can complicate or facilitate the distribution of assets. This introductory section explores the significance of family dynamics in estate planning and how they can shape the creation of a harmonious and effective estate plan.

The Influence of Family Relationships

Family dynamics play a crucial role in shaping estate plans. Relationships between spouses, siblings, children, and extended family members can influence decisions about guardianships, asset distribution, and powers of attorney. For example, in a family where there is a strong bond and trust among the members, an estate plan might straightforwardly include evenly split assets among the children. However, in families where conflicts or estrangement exist, the estate plan might require more nuanced structures, such as trusts, to specify how, when, and under what conditions assets are distributed to prevent disputes and ensure fairness.

Accounting for Complex Family Structures

Modern families often include stepchildren, half-siblings, former spouses, and second marriages, which can complicate estate planning. Each of these relationships brings its considerations and potential for conflict or misunderstanding. For instance, in blended families, ensuring that children from a previous marriage are treated fairly alongside children from a current marriage can be a sensitive issue that requires careful planning and clear communication.

Impact of Family Roles and Expectations

In many families, certain members may assume specific roles such as caregiver, financial provider, or the family mediator. These roles can lead to different expectations about what each family member believes they deserve or are entitled to from the estate. For example, a child who has taken on the role of caregiver might expect to inherit the family home or a larger share of the estate. Recognizing and addressing these roles and expectations in the estate planning process is essential to mitigate resentment and potential legal challenges.

Communication: The Bedrock of Effective Planning

Effective communication is paramount in estate planning, especially when dealing with complex family dynamics. Open discussions about estate plans can help manage expectations, clarify intentions, and avoid future disputes. It's crucial for family members to understand why certain decisions have been made, which can only be achieved through clear and honest communication. This involves discussing who will hold powers of attorney, the reasons behind the distribution of assets, and any provisions made for family members with special needs or circumstances.

Navigating Emotional Sensitivities

Estate planning can often bring to the surface underlying familial tensions and emotional sensitivities. Issues such as perceived inequality, favoritism, or past grievances can impact how family members react to the estate plan. It is important for the estate planner to approach these issues with empathy, ensuring that all family members feel heard and considered. This might involve using mediation or family meetings to address and reconcile differing views before finalizing the estate plan.

Family Dynamics Change Over Time

Everyone thinks of their family as of today. My job as an estate planning attorney is to think into the future, often decades from now, to see how your family may change over time. I spot issues of concern and educate you on their impact on your family. Then, I offer options, with the pros and cons of each option, on how to address those issues. Your family will change with births, deaths, marriages, and divorces. With changing family dynamics, your goals and wishes may change. Keeping up with changing family dynamics is important to staying current with your estate planning needs.

Give to Whom you Want, When You Want, How You Want, and Keeping the Wrong People Out

You know who you want to give your inheritance to. However, do you also want to plan when they get their inheritance, how they get it, what they can use it for, and to keep the wrong people out?

Most clients think that they will give their inheritance directly and outright to each beneficiary. Giving an inheritance directly and outright to a beneficiary could have serious and unintended consequences. Your inheritance is like a big pile of cash to the beneficiary. The beneficiary did not earn it and does appreciate that it took a lifetime to accumulate your wealth. Receiving an inheritance is like winning the lottery. Unfortunately, according to a Certified Financial Planner Board of Standards 2015 report nearly one in three lottery winners file for bankruptcy within three to five years after winning the lottery. That means that they were actually worse off than before they received the money. Many people cannot handle a big financial windfall. Friends and distant relatives come out of the woodwork. Money is spent unwisely, and before you know it the inheritance is gone, and creditors take what is left over. We need to consider the ability of each beneficiary to receive the inheritance, or whether we should protect it for them.

But giving an inheritance directly and outright to a beneficiary is not the only option. With your estate plan, you have the option to keep the inheritance money in a protective sub-trust for your beneficiary after you die. This would protect the funds from the beneficiary's creditors, a son-in-law or daughter-in-law in case of a divorce or death or prevent the beneficiary from squandering the inheritance.

Even if you have a beneficiary who is well off with a great job and doesn't need the money, you may still want to hold the inheritance in a protective sub-trust for him or her. Maybe your beneficiary is in an industry where they're prone to lawsuits or they have a high maintenance spouse. The inheritance in a protective sub-trust can set money aside for him or her away from creditors, lawsuits, or a high-spending spouse.

You may have a beneficiary who lacks financial experience in being able to manage his or her own finances or is susceptible to friends and distant relatives who might try to take their inheritance. Such a beneficiary would benefit from a protective sub-trust that would hold the inheritance money for him or her so that it will last.

You may have a beneficiary who has a troubled marriage, and we may want to protect that person's inheritance from a divorce from your son-in-law or daughter-in-law. A protective sub-trust would only benefit your child and not your son-in-law or daughter-in-law.

You may have a beneficiary who has creditors or bankruptcy issues or will spend their money on their addictions. A protective sub-trust would only benefit him or her by making sure that creditors cannot receive the inheritance and he or she doesn't have access to all of the money to spend on his or her addictions.

If you have a beneficiary with special needs, he or she may receive needs-based government assistance, such as Social Security disability (SSI), Medi-Cal, and in-home support services (IHSS), where someone comes to their home and helps them around the house. In general, to qualify for these needs-based government programs, the special needs person cannot have more than $2,000 of countable assets. Although California has eliminated the asset test for Medi-Cal benefits, if the benefits recipient moves out of California, then they would become ineligible for Medicaid in another state. If you give the inheritance money to a special needs person, then he or she would become ineligible for the needs-based government benefits because he or she would have more than $2,000 of countable assets. This could be disastrous for the needs-based government benefits to be eliminated. As a part of your estate plan, you can create a Special Needs Sub-Trust that would still allow the special needs person to qualify for the needs-based government benefits because any assets in a Special Needs Sub-Trust would not be counted towards eligibility. You would thereby provide funds for the special needs person and still preserve the needs-based government benefits.

Conclusion

Family dynamics are a critical component of estate planning that can influence the effectiveness and harmony of the plan's execution. By understanding and thoughtfully addressing the complexities of family relationships, you can create an estate plan that not only distributes assets according to legal and financial considerations but also respects and acknowledges the emotional and relational aspects of your family. This approach helps ensure a smoother transition and administration of the estate, aligning with both your wishes and the best interests of your family members.

CHAPTER 9

MARRIED COUPLES: WHAT HAPPENS WHEN THE FIRST SPOUSE PASSES AWAY?

When one spouse dies, we have to plan on what will happen to the assets of the community property and separate property, if any. Will the other spouse remarry? It is less common for a wife to remarry if her husband dies. My wife says it's because she's already trained one husband, she doesn't have the time and patience to train another husband. But it is more common for a husband to remarry after a wife dies. Men are more susceptible to being victimized by younger women and they are more likely to remarry after their wife passes away. Could your spouse be victimized? Will your children receive their inheritance? What safeguards can be put in place with an estate plan so that you know your surviving spouse will be taken care of, but that your assets will go to your children after the surviving spouse dies.

Estate Planning for Married Couples: Survivor's Trust, Bypass Trust, and QTIP Trust Options

When one spouse in a married couple passes away, the surviving spouse must make decisions about how to manage and distribute the couple's assets. Proper estate planning allows for various structures to protect assets, minimize estate taxes, and ensure that the couple's wishes are carried out. Typical estate planning tools for married couples include the creation of a Survivor's Trust, Bypass Trust, and Qualified Terminable Interest Property (QTIP) Trust. Each of these tools offers unique benefits depending on the family's needs, tax considerations, and goals.

This section will explore three primary options available to married couples when planning for the death of the first spouse: (1) leaving everything to the surviving spouse in the Survivor's Trust with an option to disclaim assets to a Bypass Trust; (2) creating a mandatory division of assets between a Survivor's Trust and a Bypass Trust; and (3) using the Clayton Election. Each of these strategies comes with its own set of pros and cons.

The Trust Options

1. Survivor's Trust

A Survivor's Trust is typically a revocable trust designed to hold the surviving spouse's share of the assets after the first spouse dies. Assets in the Survivor's Trust are fully accessible by the surviving spouse during their lifetime and can be spent, managed, or transferred at their discretion. Because the Survivor's Trust is revocable, the surviving spouse can change the beneficiaries or anything else about the trust. The Survivor's Trust uses the surviving spouse's social security number, and any income earned by the Survivor's Trust is reported on the surviving spouse's income tax return. Upon the death of the surviving spouse, the remaining assets in the trust pass to the final beneficiaries, such as children or other heirs.

2. Bypass Trust (also called a Credit Shelter Trust)

A Bypass Trust, also known as an Exemption Trust, Credit Shelter Trust, or B Trust, is an irrevocable trust established at the death of the first spouse. The primary purpose of the Bypass Trust is to shelter part of the deceased spouse's estate from estate taxes. Assets placed in the Bypass Trust do not count toward the surviving spouse's estate when the surviving spouse passes away, ensuring that the federal estate tax exemption of the first spouse is fully utilized. The surviving spouse typically has limited access to the trust's assets (often for income or principal for specific purposes like health, education, maintenance, and support). Since the Bypass Trust is irrevocable, the surviving spouse cannot amend or change the beneficiaries. The Bypass Trust will get its own Employer Identification Number (EIN) from the IRS and file its own annual income tax return. Assets in the Bypass Trust do not get a second step-up in basis upon the death of the surviving spouse.

3. Qualified Terminable Interest Property (QTIP) Trust

A QTIP Trust allows the surviving spouse to receive income from the trust for life, while the principal (or remaining assets) is preserved for the final beneficiaries, typically children. The key benefit of a QTIP Trust is that it qualifies for the estate tax marital deduction, meaning no estate taxes are due at the first spouse's death. However, the assets in the QTIP Trust are included in the surviving spouse's estate and are taxed upon their death unless other planning techniques are used. Since the QTIP Trust is irrevocable, the surviving spouse cannot amend or change the beneficiaries. The QTIP Trust will get its own EIN from the IRS and file its own annual income tax return. Upon formation, the surviving spouse must file an estate tax return to elect QTIP status for the QTIP Trust. Assets in the QTIP Trust will get a second step-up in basis upon the death of the surviving spouse.

Estate Planning Options Upon the Death of the First Spouse

Option 1: Leave All Assets to the Survivor's Trust with the Option to Disclaim into a Bypass Trust

In this option, upon the death of the first spouse, all assets are transferred into the Survivor's Trust. However, the surviving spouse retains the option to "disclaim" (refuse) some portion of the assets, which would then be transferred into an irrevocable Bypass Trust.

Pros:

- Flexibility: This option allows the surviving spouse to evaluate the family's financial situation, tax laws, and personal needs at the time of the first spouse's death. If estate tax laws or financial conditions change, the spouse can decide whether to fund the Bypass Trust.
- Tax Control: If the estate tax threshold is high and no tax is due, the surviving spouse may choose to keep all assets in the Survivor's Trust. Alternatively, if funding the Bypass Trust is necessary for estate tax planning, the surviving spouse can opt to disclaim assets to minimize taxes on the estate upon their own death. This allows for flexibility in the estate plan in the future.
- Full Control of Survivor's Trust: The surviving spouse retains full control over the assets in the Survivor's Trust and can use them for any purpose.

Cons:

- Emotional Stress: Making decisions about disclaiming assets shortly after the death of a spouse may be emotionally taxing.

- Potential for Inaction: If the surviving spouse does not act to disclaim assets in a timely manner (usually within nine months of death), the opportunity to utilize the Bypass Trust is lost.
- No Guarantee of Estate Tax Savings: If the survivor does not disclaim assets into the Bypass Trust, the full value of the estate may be included in their estate, possibly resulting in a higher estate tax burden upon their death.

Option 2: Mandatory Division of Assets Between the Survivor's Trust and a Bypass Trust

In this scenario, upon the death of the first spouse, the couple's assets are automatically divided into two portions: the survivor's separate property and half of the community property goes into the Survivor's Trust for the surviving spouse, and the deceased spouse's separate property and half of the community property is irrevocably placed into a Bypass Trust.

Pros:

- Immediate Tax Planning: The mandatory split ensures that the estate tax exemption of the first spouse is utilized at their death. This can shield a significant portion of the estate from estate taxes upon the death of the surviving spouse.
- Protection from Future Spouses: By placing assets in the Bypass Trust, you protect those assets from being accessed by a potential new spouse if the surviving spouse remarries.
- Fixed Structure: The mandatory division provides a clear and structured plan, preventing the surviving spouse from making decisions based on emotional or financial pressures.

Cons:

- Lack of Flexibility: The mandatory division lacks flexibility. If circumstances change, the surviving spouse cannot alter the division to meet their financial needs or take advantage of favorable tax laws.
- Limited Access to Bypass Trust: The surviving spouse typically has restricted access to the Bypass Trust assets (usually limited

to income or distributions for health, education, maintenance, or support), which may reduce their financial flexibility.

Option 3: The Clayton Election

The Clayton Election is a hybrid approach that allows for flexibility in allocating assets between a QTIP Trust and a Bypass Trust. Upon the death of the first spouse, the assets that would otherwise pass to the QTIP Trust can instead be directed to the Bypass Trust if the surviving spouse (or trustee) makes this election on the estate tax return.

Pros:

- Tax Deferral with Flexibility: This option allows the surviving spouse (or trustee) to defer estate taxes by using the QTIP marital deduction but still retain the flexibility to divert assets to the Bypass Trust if tax considerations change.
- Flexibility After Death: The decision to fund the Bypass Trust or the QTIP Trust can be made after the first spouse's death, allowing for tax and financial considerations at the time to influence the choice.
- Potential for Estate Tax Savings: The election allows the surviving spouse to utilize the first spouse's estate tax exemption by directing assets to the Bypass Trust, which can minimize the overall estate tax burden.

Cons:

- Complexity: The Clayton Election requires careful planning and coordination with the estate tax return. It may be more complex to implement than a straightforward Survivor's Trust or mandatory division.
- Uncertainty: The surviving spouse or trustee has the power to choose where the assets go, which could lead to uncertainty or family conflicts if beneficiaries disagree with the decisions made.

Conclusion

Each of these options offers a different balance between flexibility, tax planning, and control over the assets. Choosing the right approach depends on the family's financial situation, goals for protecting the surviving spouse, and priorities for minimizing estate taxes. Regularly reviewing the estate plan with an attorney is essential to ensure it remains aligned with current laws and personal needs.

CHAPTER 10
FAMILIES WITH MINOR CHILDREN

Estate Planning for Families with Minor Children

Estate planning for families with young children under 18 years of age carries unique considerations and responsibilities. The primary goal for parents in this situation is to ensure their children are cared for and protected in the event that something happens to them.

A minor is anyone who is under the age of 18. Minor children cannot care for themselves and will need someone to live with if their parents are both gone. You will need to nominate guardians to step in as substitute parents to take care of your children. But who will handle the children's money, and should that person be the same person that they live with? Do you have any special instructions for your minor children? Should encouraging college, vocational school, or other higher education be a goal? When will your minor children receive their inheritance? These are some of the questions that need to be addressed in the estate planning process.

The Issue with Minor Children

You cannot give a minor assets directly because they are not legally able to buy or sell real estate, enter into contracts, or transact with financial accounts. Without an estate plan, there may need to be a guardianship, which is a court procedure to appoint a guardian over the minor child and manage his or her money. Guardianship is an expensive, intrusive, and time-consuming court procedure that requires regular court filings and accountings.

To prevent the need for a guardianship for the inheritance of a minor child, the funds can be kept in a protective sub-trust for the child's benefit. Your Successor Trustee would manage the finances and provide for the minor child as needed. The protective sub-trust would allow for distributions from the trust for the health, education, maintenance, or support of a child, and you could also determine how and when they will receive their inheritance in the future.

If you leave your inheritance to a minor without proper planning, they will receive their inheritance when they turn 18 years old. At that age, many young adults may not have the financial maturity to manage a large sum of money, potentially wasting it on impractical expenses. To avoid this, you may choose to give them their assets in stages, such as a third at age 18, a third at age 25, and the final third at age 30. Alternatively, the inheritance could be held in trust for their lifetime, with distributions made for their health, education, maintenance, and support.

Designating Guardians for Minor Children

One of the most critical decisions for parents is choosing a guardian for their young children. This involves legally appointing someone to take on the responsibility of raising the children if both parents were to pass away or become incapacitated. This decision must be made with great care, considering the potential guardian's values, parenting style, stability, and emotional bond with the children.

Creating Trusts for Minor Children

Parents may choose to establish trusts to manage any assets that children would inherit until they are old enough to manage these assets themselves. A trust can specify at what age children will receive their inheritance, or it can release funds in increments at different ages or milestones (such as graduating from college). Many families choose to leave the funds in trust for their children's lifetimes. Trusts can also dictate how the funds should be used, such as for education, healthcare, or general support.

Life Insurance for Minor Children

Having adequate life insurance is crucial for parents with young children. Life insurance can provide financial support that substitutes for the income or care that a parent provides. It can help cover daily living expenses, educational costs, and any other child-rearing expenses if one or both parents pass away. Parents should consider the amount of life insurance needed based on their current lifestyle, future needs, and any outstanding debts that might impact their children's financial future.

Appointing Financial Guardians or Trustees

In addition to naming a personal guardian who will raise the minor children, parents should consider appointing a financial guardian or trustee. A minor child cannot manage their own financial accounts, and an adult must oversee these funds. This role can be assigned to the same person as the personal guardian or to someone else, providing an opportunity for checks and balances.

For example, if the personal guardian has their own young children, it might be wise to appoint a different person as the financial guardian to ensure that the inheritance intended for your children is not used for the guardian's own family. The financial guardian or trustee's responsibility is to manage the inheritance in accordance with your wishes, ensuring the children's financial needs are met properly.

Instructions for Care and Values Education

Beyond the legal and financial aspects of estate planning, parents may choose to leave written instructions about the upbringing, education, and values they wish their children to receive. These instructions can help guide the guardian in raising the children and ensure that family values or educational aspirations are upheld.

Regular Updates to the Estate Plan

As children grow and circumstances change, it is important for parents to update their estate plans. What may have been suitable when a child was a toddler may no longer be appropriate when they are teenagers. Regular reviews and updates help ensure that the estate plan remains relevant and effective.

Summary

Estate planning for families with young children involves unique considerations, from appointing guardians and financial trustees to creating trusts for asset management. By addressing these aspects in their estate plans, parents can ensure their children's security and well-being in almost any eventuality. This proactive approach provides peace of mind, knowing that children will be cared for according to their parents' wishes, and helps to avoid the potential pitfalls of leaving large inheritances to young adults who may not yet be financially responsible.

CHAPTER 11
BLENDED FAMILIES

Estate planning for blended families—those in which one or both partners bring children from previous relationships into the marriage—presents unique challenges and requires careful consideration to ensure that all members are treated fairly and according to the parents' wishes. Blended family dynamics can significantly influence how estate plans are structured to avoid potential conflicts and ensure that no family member feels overlooked.

A blended family is one where there are children not of the marriage. The children can be his, hers and ours. A major issue of a blended family is having both separate and community property of the spouses. Who should get what assets? A blended family presents unique estate planning challenges.

Another major issue of a blended family is who the heirs are of each spouse. According to the California laws of intestate succession, the heirs of each spouse are only their own biological children, not their stepchildren. In the event that one spouse dies, the children of the deceased spouse could be unintentionally disinherited when the surviving spouse receives all of the assets.

How can you make sure that the children of both spouses are treated fairly? What options are available to plan for a blended family? Which of the options is best for your family, your assets, and your particular situation?

Not all of my estate planning clients have a blended family, but their adult children are in blended families. How can their estate plan take that into consideration?

You may not have a blended family now, but you may have a blended family in the future.

Consider what would happen if one spouse were to pass away and the other was to remarry. What protections should we put into place to avoid the surviving spouse being susceptible to being victimized or to protect the inheritance or the children? No one wants their assets to go to their replacement.

If you have a blended family, consider what would happen if one parent passed away.

Your stepchildren are not your heirs. Likewise, your children are not their stepparent's heirs. If we want to plan for a blended family, we have to take some special considerations into account to treat all children fairly. It's common for a stepmother or stepfather to not have a great relationship with their stepchildren and want to treat them as their own children. In other families, there is tension between stepparents and stepchildren. Understanding the issues of blended families and learning the options available is a big step in determining how to do make sure that all children and stepchildren receive their inheritance.

Unique Challenges in Blended Families

1. Protecting the Rights of Both Biological and Stepchildren: One of the primary concerns in blended families is ensuring that both biological and stepchildren are considered in the estate plan. Parents need to balance the needs of their children from previous relationships with those of any new spouse or stepchildren.
2. Managing Different Financial Needs and Expectations: Different family members may have varying financial needs and expectations, which can create potential for conflict. For example, older children who may have been self-sufficient longer could have different expectations about what they should receive compared to much younger stepchildren still living at home.
3. Dealing with Previous Spouses: Previous spouses can complicate estate planning, especially if there are ongoing financial obligations such as alimony or child support. Ensuring these are addressed in the estate plan is crucial.

Strategies for Estate Planning in Blended Families

1. Clear Wills and Trusts: It is essential to create clear, legally binding documents that specify how assets are to be divided among the surviving spouse, biological children, and stepchildren. Trusts can be particularly useful in blended families to allocate resources to the surviving spouse for the duration of their life and then pass the remaining assets to the children from previous marriages.
2. Designation of Beneficiaries: Properly designating beneficiaries for life insurance policies, retirement accounts, and other financial assets is crucial. These designations should be regularly reviewed and updated to reflect any changes in the

family structure, such as the birth of additional children or a new marriage.

3. Use of Marital Agreements: Pre-nuptial or post-nuptial agreements can define community property vs. separate property and what will happen to each partner's assets in the event of death or divorce, which can be particularly important in protecting the interests of children from previous relationships.
4. Flexible Trust Structures: Trusts can be designed to offer flexibility and address the specific needs of blended families. For example, a Bypass trust can provide income to a surviving spouse while preserving the principal for children from a previous marriage.
5. Equalization of Inheritances: Sometimes, one part of the family might have received more benefits during the parent's lifetime (such as living in a family business or receiving a paid-for education). Estate planning can balance these benefits by adjusting inheritances so that all children feel they are treated fairly.
6. Communication and Transparency: Open dialogue about estate planning decisions is crucial in blended families. It helps manage expectations and reduces the potential for conflict after the parent's death. Parents should explain their decisions to all family members to ensure that everyone understands their reasoning.

Conclusion

For blended families, the goal of estate planning is to honor the relationships and provide for the future of all family members—spouses, biological children, and stepchildren alike. It requires careful and thoughtful planning, consideration of all family members' emotions and financial needs, and often, the assistance of an experienced estate planning attorney to navigate the complex legal landscape.

CHAPTER 12

KEEPING YOUR INHERITANCE WITHIN YOUR BLOODLINE

Estate Planning to Keep Inheritance Within the Bloodline

Keeping an inheritance within the bloodline is a common goal in estate planning, especially in families seeking to preserve wealth across generations or protect assets from potential external claims such as divorces or lawsuits.

Everyone knows who they want to give their inheritance to. But a good estate plan can also give when you want, how you want, and *keep the wrong people out.*

Here are key considerations and strategies to ensure that assets remain within the bloodline and are protected from outside influences.

Key Concerns in Bloodline Estate Planning

1. Marital Dissolution: One of the main risks to bloodline preservation is the potential for assets to become subject to division in marital dissolution. If an heir divorces, without proper safeguards, a significant portion of their inherited wealth could be claimed by the ex-spouse.
2. Creditor Claims: Inheritances can be vulnerable to creditor claims against heirs. If an heir incurs significant debts, creditors might target inherited assets as a repayment source.
3. Mismanagement by Heirs: Sometimes, heirs may not have the skill or experience to manage substantial inherited wealth, which could lead to rapid depletion of the assets through poor investments or extravagant spending.

Strategies to Keep Assets Within the Bloodline

1. Use of Trusts: Trusts are the most effective tool for ensuring that assets remain within the bloodline. You can set up various types of trusts, depending on your specific goals:

   - Discretionary Trusts: These trusts give the trustee broad discretion in distributing assets and income among various beneficiaries, which can protect the trust's assets from being directly accessed by creditors or in a divorce.
   - Spendthrift Trusts: This type of trust includes a spendthrift clause that restricts the beneficiaries' ability to pledge, sell, or otherwise dispose of their interest in the trust assets, protecting the assets from creditors.
   - Dynasty Trusts: Designed to last for multiple generations, dynasty trusts can help in preserving wealth within the family by imposing strict stipulations on distributions, thereby ensuring that assets pass on from one generation to the next without being subject to estate taxes at each transfer.

2. Prenuptial and Postnuptial Agreements: Encouraging or requiring heirs to enter into prenuptial or postnuptial

agreements can protect inherited assets in the event of a divorce. These agreements can specify that inherited assets are not considered marital property and are therefore excluded from any division of assets.

3. Titling of Assets: Properly titling assets is crucial. Ensure that inherited assets are registered in the name of the trust or explicitly designated as separate property, not commingled with marital assets, to avoid them becoming subject to division in a divorce.
4. Family Limited Partnerships (FLPs) or LLCs: Creating a family limited partnership or a family LLC can be an effective way to hold family assets, providing control over assets to senior family members and limiting transfer rights. This can prevent heirs from transferring their shares without family consent, thus keeping assets within the family.
5. Education and Family Governance: Educating heirs about the value of wealth preservation and establishing strong family governance can encourage responsible stewardship of assets. Family meetings, estate planning workshops, and involving heirs in the estate planning process can foster a sense of responsibility and continuity.

Conclusion

To keep an inheritance within the bloodline and shield it from external risks, it's vital to deploy a combination of legal structures, agreements, and family education. Trusts, properly drafted and maintained, serve as the cornerstone of such planning, complemented by prenuptial agreements and careful asset management strategies. Regularly reviewing and updating your estate plan with an experienced attorney can also ensure that your objectives are met as family circumstances and laws evolve. This comprehensive approach can help preserve your family's wealth and legacy for generations to come.

CHAPTER 13
PREVENTING YOUR IN-LAWS FROM BEING OUT-LAWS

How Your Daughter-In-Law May Get Your Inheritance

This possibility catches many people off-guard. Image that after you die, you give your inheritance directly and outright to your son. His wife (your daughter-in-law) asks him, "Honey, did you get your parent's inheritance?" He replies, "Yes, Dear. I got it." She says, "Well, I checked with the bank about our joint checking account, and they don't have a deposit. Do you think they made a mistake?" That question puts your son in the most awkward conversation that he can have with his wife. Your son can't tell his wife, "I love you, but my parents didn't work hard their entire lives... sacrificing and saving up money to leave an inheritance to me all so that you can take it to buy jewelry, designer shoes, and handbags!" So, he puts the money in a joint bank account with your daughter-in-law. Now she has access to the money to spend it on jewelry, designer shoes, and handbags.

Estate Planning to Protect Inheritance from Misuse

When crafting an estate plan, one common concern among parents is ensuring that the inheritance they leave for their children is used responsibly and protected from potential misuse, such as a child's spouse spending it on extravagant, non-essential items. This situation can be particularly delicate if you are concerned about a daughter-in-law or son-in-law who may not share your values regarding financial management or the intended use of the family wealth. Here are some strategic approaches to consider in estate planning to address these concerns.

Understanding the Risks

1. Dissipation of Assets: If an heir's spouse has expensive tastes or habits, like purchasing designer shoes and purses, there's a risk that the inheritance could be quickly depleted on these luxury items, leaving little for more substantial needs or future generations.
2. Marital Dissolution: If the marriage of your son ends in divorce, assets that have been commingled with marital property could be divided with the spouse, potentially reducing the amount that remains within your immediate family.

Estate Planning Strategies

1. Creating a Trust: A trust is a powerful tool for controlling how and when your assets are distributed after your death. Consider setting up a trust with specific terms that dictate how the inheritance can be used. For example:
    - Discretionary Trust: This allows the trustee to have control over the distribution of assets, providing funds for necessities and beneficial activities (like education or

business investments) while limiting access to funds for frivolous expenditures.

- Incentive Trust: This type of trust can set conditions for disbursements based on behavior or achievements, such as matching funds for earnings or releasing funds only for educational purposes.

2. Appointing a Trustworthy Trustee: Choose a trustee who understands your family dynamics and financial goals. This could be another family member, a trusted friend, a professional trustee, or a trust company who can impartially manage the trust according to your wishes.
3. Spendthrift Clause: Including a spendthrift clause in the trust can prevent heirs and their creditors (including divorcing spouses) from accessing trust funds beyond what the trust allows to be distributed. This legally restricts the beneficiary's ability to pledge the trust's assets as collateral or to assign their interest to others.
4. Clear Communication: It's often beneficial to have open discussions about financial responsibility and inheritance expectations with your children and their spouses. While this can be sensitive, clear communication about the purpose of the inheritance and your intentions can sometimes mitigate misunderstandings and imprudent spending.
5. Separate Accounts and Titling: Encourage your children to keep their inheritance in separate accounts titled only in their names. This can help ensure that the inheritance is legally recognized as separate property, not subject to division in a divorce.
6. Prenuptial Agreements: If your son is not yet married or considering a subsequent marriage, discussing the importance of a prenuptial agreement can be prudent. Such agreements can specify that an inheritance remains separate property in the event of a divorce.

Conclusion

Protecting an inheritance from being misused by a family member's spouse involves careful planning and legal safeguards. By utilizing trusts, clear family communication, and legal arrangements like prenuptial agreements, you can help ensure that your wealth is preserved for its intended purposes. Consulting with an estate planning attorney to implement these strategies effectively is crucial, as they can provide tailored advice and solutions that align with your family's needs and values.

CHAPTER 14

PROTECTING YOUR CHILDREN'S INHERITANCE FROM THEIR CREDITORS, LAWSUITS, OR BANKRUPTCY

Estate Planning to Protect Inheritance from Creditors, Lawsuits, or Bankruptcy

Protecting an inheritance from creditors, lawsuits, or bankruptcy is a significant concern for many families in estate planning. This concern involves ensuring that the wealth passed on to heirs remains safeguarded against external claims, potentially arising from business failures, professional liabilities, accidents, or financial mismanagement. Here are several strategies that can be employed to ensure that your child's inheritance is protected from such vulnerabilities.

Understanding the Risks

1. Creditors' Claims: If an heir has significant debts, creditors might target their inheritance as a source for repayment.
2. Legal Judgments: If your child is sued for any reason, such as a personal injury lawsuit, any inherited assets held in their name could be at risk in a judgment.
3. Bankruptcy: Should your child declare bankruptcy; their inheritance could be used to satisfy bankruptcy claims unless adequately protected.

Estate Planning Strategies

1. Use of Trusts: Trusts are a fundamental tool in asset protection planning. They can shield inherited assets from the beneficiaries' creditors, lawsuits, and bankruptcy proceedings by placing a legal barrier between the beneficiary and the assets.

    - Discretionary Trusts: These trusts provide the trustee with the authority to decide when and how much the beneficiary receives, offering no guaranteed income or asset that creditors can claim.
    - Spendthrift Trusts: Incorporating a spendthrift clause can restrict the beneficiary's ability to assign future distributions to creditors or others. This clause explicitly protects trust assets from being claimed by creditors.
    - Asset Protection Trusts: Some jurisdictions allow for the creation of asset protection trusts that, if properly structured and administered, can provide robust protection against creditors and legal judgments.

2. Retirement Accounts: Encourage your child to maximize contributions to retirement accounts such as IRAs and 401(k) s, which often enjoy protection from creditors under state and federal law.
3. Titling of Assets: Advising on the titling of assets can also protect wealth. Assets held as community property, available

only to married couples, may protect the assets from capital gains tax after the first spouse to pass away.

4. Life Insurance and Annuities: In many states, life insurance policies and annuities can be payable to the trust so that your beneficiaries have their funds protected from their creditors.
5. Homestead Exemption: The automatic homestead in California only offers limited protections in case you are forced to sell your primary residence. If you want to sell your home and keep the equity in your home from judgement liens, then you must record a declaration of homestead to protect your primary residence from certain types of judgement liens.
6. Prenuptial Agreements: If your child is married or plans to marry, consider the benefits of a prenuptial agreement to segregate inherited assets from marital property, which can be vulnerable in divorce proceedings.

Legal Considerations and Compliance

- Timeliness: It's crucial that these protective strategies are implemented before any issues arise. Actions taken to protect assets after a claim arises can be seen as fraudulent transfers and thereby not avoid the creditors.
- Compliance with Laws: Ensure that all strategies comply with state and federal laws. Consulting with an estate planning or asset protection attorney is recommended to tailor strategies to specific circumstances and legal requirements.

Conclusion

Protecting your children's inheritance from creditors, lawsuits, or bankruptcy requires thoughtful planning and strategic use of legal tools. By utilizing trusts, appropriate asset titling, and other protective mechanisms, you can help secure your child's financial future against potential external threats. Regular reviews and updates of your estate plan, in consultation with legal professionals, will also ensure that these protections remain effective over time.

CHAPTER 15

MANAGING YOUR CHILDREN'S SPENDTHRIFT TENDENCIES

Protecting Your Children's Inheritance: Strategies for Managing Spendthrift Tendencies

Estate planning is not only about deciding who should receive your assets but also about ensuring those assets are used wisely. This is particularly crucial when you're concerned that your children might not have the maturity or financial acumen to manage a significant inheritance responsibly. Whether they are very young, inexperienced with money, or known for their spendthrift habits, there are strategic ways to protect them—and their inheritance—from potential financial missteps.

Understanding the Challenges

In many ways, receiving an inheritance is like getting a new tube of toothpaste. When I first open a new tube of toothpaste, I'm wasteful and I put a lot of toothpaste on my toothbrush. I may even drop some toothpaste in the sink, but I just put more toothpaste on my toothbrush. Then, when I have very little toothpaste left in the tube, I become more careful about how much toothpaste I use. I sparingly put just enough toothpaste on my toothbrush. I even squeeze the tube to get every last bit of toothpaste out.

Similarly, the inheritance that you leave for your children is a big pile of money that your children receive after you pass away. Your children didn't work hard, sacrifice, and save to earn those funds, which gives them a lack of value for the money. They may lack the discipline and knowledge of how to handle money. The lack of value, discipline, and knowledge of how to handle the money makes it easier to spend the money wildly.

1. Young Children: Very young children obviously cannot manage assets. An 18-year-old who inherits a large sum on money goes to the nearest new car dealer to buy a fast car, every time. The primary concern here is ensuring the assets are still available and well-managed as they reach adulthood.
2. Inexperienced Children: Older children or young adults might lack the financial literacy to manage large sums of money wisely, potentially leading to poor investment choices or excessive spending. If your child wanted to take the inheritance money to take their friends on a vacation to Cancun, you'd say, "No." Why should it be different after you're gone?
3. Spendthrift Children: Some children, regardless of age, may have established patterns of irresponsible spending. Without safeguards, an inheritance could quickly be depleted on frivolous or short-term gratifications. One of the worst things that your child could buy is a yacht, that not only is expensive to buy but expensive to maintain with annual maintenance costs of up to 20% of the purchase price per year.

Estate Planning Tools and Techniques

You want your children to have the use and benefit of the inheritance that you leave to them, without it being wasted or taken from your children. You can set up the trust to provide for rent, mortgage payments, utilities, health insurance premiums, etc. for the living expenses of our children. Instead of giving the money directly to your children, the successor trustee will pay their bills for them.

1. Staggered Distributions:

Implementing staggered distributions through a trust can spread out the inheritance over several years or key milestones. For instance, the trust could dictate that the child receives a portion of the inheritance at age 25, another part at 30, and the rest at 35. Each distribution could also be tied to specific life achievements, like graduating from college or purchasing a first home.

2. Incentive Trusts:

An incentive trust can be designed to disburse funds only when certain predefined conditions are met. These conditions can be positive, such as completing a degree, maintaining employment, or making matching contributions to a retirement account. This type of trust encourages responsible behavior and helps ensure the inheritance promotes productive life choices.

3. Spendthrift Trusts:

A spendthrift trust includes a clause that protects the trust's assets from the beneficiary's creditors as well as from the beneficiary's own poor spending habits. By restricting the beneficiary's access to the trust funds, except through the specific distributions set out in the trust, you can prevent creditors from seizing the assets and the beneficiary from squandering them.

4. Discretionary Trusts:

This type of trust gives the trustee broad discretion to determine how much money to distribute to the beneficiary and when. The trustee can assess the situation and make distributions based on what they believe is in the best interest of the beneficiary, potentially withholding funds if the beneficiary is going through a phase of reckless spending.

5. Professional Financial Guidance:

Incorporating terms within the trust that require or encourage the beneficiary to consult with a financial advisor can help instill financial literacy and planning skills. The trust can even allocate funds specifically for the purpose of paying for financial advice.

6. Testamentary Trusts for Young Children:

For very young children, a testamentary trust (a trust established upon the death of the parent via the parent's will) can be particularly useful. You can appoint a trustee to manage the assets and make discretionary decisions about distributing the funds for the child's health, education, maintenance, and support until the child is capable of managing the assets themselves.

Legal and Practical Considerations

- Choose Trustees Wisely: The choice of trustee is crucial, especially if the trust grants them considerable discretion. Choose someone who is not only trustworthy but also financially savvy and ideally familiar with the family dynamics.
- Communicate Intentions: It's beneficial to discuss your plans and intentions with your children if they are old enough to understand. This can help set expectations and encourage them to think about their financial future.
- Review and Adjust: As children grow and their situations change, the terms of the trust may need to be adjusted. Regular reviews with your estate planning attorney can ensure that the trust continues to meet its intended goals.

Conclusion

By carefully considering the maturity and financial knowledge of your children, you can structure their inheritance in a way that protects them from potential financial harm. Using trusts tailored to your family's needs can provide both flexibility and control, helping to ensure that your wealth has a positive impact on your children's lives.

CHAPTER 16
ADDRESSING A CHILD'S ALCOHOL ABUSE, SUBSTANCE ABUSE, AND GAMBLING ADDICTIONS

Addressing Alcohol Abuse, Substance Abuse, and Gambling Addictions in Estate Planning

When creating an estate plan, additional care is needed when you are concerned about a child who struggles with alcohol, drug, or gambling addictions. The risk here is not only financial imprudence but also exacerbating their health and lifestyle problems through sudden wealth. Here are enhanced strategies to protect both the child and their inheritance, ensuring that the inheritance supports recovery and a healthy lifestyle rather than contributing to further destructive behavior.

Understanding the Challenges

Children struggling with addiction face unique risks when inheriting wealth:

1. Exacerbation of Addictive Behaviors: Sudden access to a large amount of money can lead to a relapse or worsening of addictive behaviors. It's crucial that the inheritance does not become a means to fund these habits.
2. Vulnerability to Exploitation: Individuals with addiction issues are often more vulnerable to being exploited financially by those who might encourage or facilitate their addiction.

Tailored Estate Planning Strategies

1. Incentive Trust with Recovery Conditions:

An incentive trust can include conditions related to the child's recovery and maintenance of sobriety. Distributions can be contingent upon the child remaining drug-free as evidenced by regular testing, attending therapy sessions, or maintaining a steady involvement in recovery programs such as Alcoholics Anonymous or similar support groups.

2. Special Purpose Trusts:

A special purpose trust can be set up specifically to manage the funds necessary for treatment and recovery. This trust can pay directly for rehabilitation services, medical treatment, counseling, and any other health-related expenses without giving cash directly to the beneficiary, thereby preventing the misuse of funds.

3. Discretionary Trusts Managed by a Professional:

A discretionary trust managed by a professional trustee (such as a bank or a professional fiduciary) can help in making objective decisions about the distribution of assets. This removes emotional decision-making from the process and places the responsibility in the hands of someone with no personal ties to the beneficiary, who can strictly adhere to the guidelines set forth in the trust.

4. Delayed Distribution:

Delaying the distribution of the inheritance until the child reaches a milestone in their recovery or a certain age can be effective. This delay allows time for maturity and potentially for gaining better control over their addiction.

5. Paying Bills and Living Expenses:

The trustee of the trust can directly pay the bills and living expenses, such as rent, utilities, health insurance premiums, etc., from the trust instead of giving the beneficiary cash to pay those expenses. This ensures that the funds are used for their intended purpose and it's very easy to set up automatic payments from the trust bank account.

6. Health and Education Trusts:

Establishing a trust specifically for educational and health-related expenses can ensure that the child has access to educational opportunities and healthcare support. These trusts restrict the use of funds to specific types of expenses, which support personal growth and development.

7. Pre-Paid Debit Cards:

Pre-paid debit cards have become very sophisticated. You now can load them up with as much or as little money as you want or set up for an automatic amount to be loaded on at set intervals. And most importantly, you can restrict where or on what the funds can be used for. A pre-paid debit card can allow small amounts of money to be released to cover daily living expenses under strict conditions, with oversight from a trustee or an appointed guardian who can monitor the spending and overall well-being of the beneficiary.

Additional Legal and Emotional Considerations

Appointment of a Guardian or Conservator: For adult children with severe addiction issues, it might be necessary to appoint a legal guardian or conservator to manage their affairs and make decisions on their behalf.

- Therapeutic Mediation: Involving a professional mediator who specializes in family and addiction issues during the estate planning process can help address sensitive topics and facilitate a healthier dialogue about the future management of the estate.
- Regular Review and Flexibility: Addiction is often a long-term issue with many ups and downs. Regularly reviewing the estate plan—with the flexibility to make adjustments as circumstances change—is crucial.

Conclusion

Estate planning for a child with addiction issues requires a careful, thoughtful approach that balances financial support with safeguards to prevent harm. By using trusts, professional trustees, and specific conditions tied to recovery, you can help ensure that your child's inheritance contributes positively to their well-being and recovery. This approach not only protects your child from potential financial misuse but also supports their journey toward a healthier life.

CHAPTER 17
SAFEGUARDING YOUR INHERITANCE FOR FUTURE GENERATIONS

How Your Inheritance Can Go Out Of Your Bloodline

We talked previously about how your daughter-in-law could end up spending the funds if your son puts his inheritance in a joint bank account with her. Let's imagine a similar but different scenario.

Imagine that after you die, you give your inheritance directly and outright to your daughter. She puts the money in a joint bank account with her husband. If she dies, then he gets it all as the joint account holder. He might be the father of her children, but he can still remarry and spend the money on his new wife or her kids. And worst of all, your grandchildren have to deal with a stepmother spending their inheritance and they may not get all of their money.

Estate Planning to Safeguard Inheritance for Future Generations

The scenario described highlights a common concern in estate planning: ensuring that an inheritance benefits your direct descendants, particularly grandchildren, even after unforeseen changes in family dynamics, such as a child's death followed by a surviving spouse's remarriage. Proper planning is essential to protect the inheritance from being diluted or redirected outside the intended family line due to these changes. Here are strategies to ensure that assets are preserved for your grandchildren, even in complex family situations.

The Risks of Direct and Unrestricted Inheritance

When you leave an inheritance directly to your daughter without restrictions, the assets become part of her estate. This means that upon her death, those assets are subject to her will or—absent a will—the state's intestacy laws, which typically would allocate the estate to her surviving spouse. This can result in unintended consequences, particularly if the surviving spouse remarries, potentially diverting the inheritance away from your grandchildren.

Strategies for Protecting Your Grandchildren's Inheritance

1. Testamentary Trusts:

Establish a Testamentary Trust in your will for your daughter that becomes effective upon your death. The trust can specify that upon her death, the remaining assets are to be used for the benefit of her children (your grandchildren). This prevents the assets from being controlled by her husband or from becoming part of any marital estate that could be accessed by a new spouse.

2. Staggered Distributions:

Instead of a lump sum, your estate plan can include "staggered distributions" at various ages or milestones, reducing the impact of potential mismanagement by either your daughter or her spouse. This can also include provisions for further distributions to your grandchildren or into a trust for their benefit after their mother's death.

3. Spendthrift Trust:

Creating a spendthrift trust for the benefit of your daughter can protect the inheritance from potential creditors, a divorcing spouse, or other claimants. A trustee would control the distribution of funds, providing for your daughter's needs while protecting the principal from being depleted. Upon her death, the trust can direct the remaining assets to her children.

4. Special Needs Trust:

If any grandchildren have special needs, a special needs trust can be established either directly or as a subtrust upon your daughter's death. This ensures that the inheritance contributes to the grandchild's care and quality of life without jeopardizing eligibility for government benefits.

5. Letter of Wishes:

Accompany your trust with a letter of wishes that provides non-binding guidance to the trustee on how you hope the trust will be administered. While not legally enforceable, it can help ensure your intentions are clear.

6. Life Insurance:

Consider taking out a life insurance policy with the trust as the beneficiary. This ensures that there are additional protected funds specifically for the benefit of your grandchildren.

7. Selection of Trustee:

Carefully consider who you choose as trustee, opting perhaps for an independent trustee (such as a trusted attorney or financial advisor) if you have concerns about family members respecting the intent of the trust.

Conclusion

These estate planning strategies are designed to ensure that your assets are preserved for the benefit of your grandchildren and protected from diversion through remarriage or other family changes after your daughter's death. By using trusts and clear directives, you can significantly reduce the risk that your estate will be misused or mishandled, ensuring that your legacy supports your descendants as you intend. Regular reviews and updates with an estate planning professional can further safeguard your intentions as family circumstances evolve.

CHAPTER 18

UNMARRIED COUPLES LIVING TOGETHER

With a single person household, the client is not married. One potential legal issue comes up when the single person lives with a significant other. The live-in partner could gain a one-half interest in the client's assets, even though they are not married. This was the California Supreme Court decision in the case of *Marvin v. Marvin* (1976) 18 Cal.3d 660.

Unmarried couples living together face unique estate planning challenges compared to their married counterparts. Without the legal framework of marriage, these couples must take specific legal steps to ensure their estate planning wishes are recognized and enforced.

The property rights of unmarried couples living together

The California Supreme Court case of *Marvin v. Marvin* (1976) 18 Cal.3d 660 is particularly significant for unmarried couples living together in California. In this landmark decision, the California Supreme Court recognized that unmarried partners may have the right to enforce express or implied agreements regarding the division of property upon the termination of their relationship. This case stemmed from Best Actor Oscar-winner (1965 Cat Ballou) Lee Marvin's relationship with Michelle Triola Marvin (they weren't married, but she had changed her last name to Marvin). They had an oral agreement that they would share their home, that Lee would take care of Michelle financially so she could stop working as an entertainer and signer. In relying on Lee's promise, Michelle gave up her career. Even though they were not married, even though there is no common law marriage in California, the court ruled that while cohabitating partners are not entitled to the same property rights as spouses, they can still establish agreements that must be honored, similar to business partnerships. Michelle Marvin was entitled to half of Lee Marvin's assets, as if they were married.

Key Points from Marvin v. Marvin:

- **Express or Implied Contracts:** Unmarried partners can enter into agreements that dictate how their property is to be handled both during and after their relationship.
- **Enforcement of Agreements:** Courts can enforce these agreements if they find them to be fair and supported by evidence.
- **No Automatic Rights:** The case underscores that cohabitants do not automatically acquire rights typical of spouses, emphasizing the importance of drafting clear agreements.

Lack of Automatic Rights

Unlike married couples, unmarried partners do not automatically inherit each other's assets unless specified in a will or other legal document. This absence of automatic succession rights can lead to significant hardships if one partner dies without a comprehensive estate plan.

Healthcare Decisions

Unmarried couples generally do not have the right to make healthcare decisions for each other unless they have executed durable powers of attorney for healthcare that explicitly grant them this authority.

Retirement Benefits and Social Security:

Unmarried couples may not be entitled to receive each other's retirement benefits or Social Security survivor benefits, which are typically reserved for spouses.

Conclusion

For unmarried couples, proactive estate planning is essential to secure their financial futures and personal wishes. The principles established in *Marvin v. Marvin* offer a legal basis for these couples to create enforceable agreements regarding their property and support obligations, which is crucial in the absence of marriage. This case highlights the need for clear communication and legal documentation in managing the complex issues associated with estate planning for unmarried couples.

CHAPTER 19
WILL YOUR SPOUSE REMARRY AFTER YOU'RE GONE?

Estate Planning Concerns Regarding Spousal Remarriage

One significant concern in estate planning is the possibility of a surviving spouse remarrying after the death of their partner. This situation can have substantial implications on the distribution of your estate, affecting not just the surviving spouse but also any children or other beneficiaries designated in your initial estate plan. Understanding and planning for these potential changes is crucial to ensure that your assets are distributed according to your wishes and that your heirs are protected.

I have a client who is in his mid-80's and his wife of over 50 years died. He found himself newly single. He is worried that younger women in their 60's are coming after him. One of them is a yoga instructor and has made it clear that she is looking for someone to take care of her. Golddiggers and opportunists are out there, and you have to be careful of being a target.

Impact of Remarriage on Estate Distribution

1. Risk to Children's Inheritance: One of the primary concerns is that the assets intended for your children (or other beneficiaries) might become compromised if the surviving spouse remarries. Assets left directly to a spouse might legally become part of their marital property in the new relationship, potentially subject to division in subsequent divorce proceedings or passing to the new spouse upon their death.
2. Dilution of the Surviving Spouse's Estate: Without specific safeguards, a significant portion of your estate intended for your surviving spouse might end up benefiting the new partner or their children, rather than your own children or designated beneficiaries.
3. Legal Complications: Remarriage can introduce various legal complexities, including changes in the surviving spouse's financial and legal status, which could impact tax liabilities and inheritance structures.

Strategies to Mitigate the Effects of Remarriage

1. Use of Trusts: Establishing a trust can be an effective way to provide for a surviving spouse while protecting the principal assets for future distribution to your own children or designated beneficiaries. A common tool is the Qualified Terminable Interest Property (QTIP) trust, which allows the surviving spouse to receive income from the trust during their lifetime, with the remainder of the trust assets passing to other beneficiaries upon their death.
2. Prenuptial Agreements: Encouraging or arranging for a surviving spouse to sign a prenuptial agreement before remarrying can help ensure that the assets from the first marriage are not commingled with the marital property of

the new marriage, protecting them from division in potential subsequent divorce settlements.

3. Specific Bequests and Conditional Gifts: Your estate plan can include specific bequests to your children or other beneficiaries that bypass your surviving spouse, or conditional gifts that depend on the spouse not remarrying.
4. Life Insurance: Setting up a life insurance policy with your children or other beneficiaries as the beneficiaries can provide them with financial security independent of the assets left to the surviving spouse.
5. Regular Reviews and Updates of the Estate Plan: Encourage regular reviews of estate plans following significant life changes, such as the death of a spouse or their remarriage. This ensures that the estate plan remains aligned with your wishes and adapts to new circumstances.

Conclusion

Considering the possibility of a spouse remarrying after your death is a critical aspect of comprehensive estate planning. It requires careful structuring of asset distribution strategies to protect your estate's integrity and ensure that your intentions are honored. By utilizing trusts, encouraging prenuptial agreements, and making specific bequests, you can safeguard your assets from unintended redistribution while providing for your spouse and protecting your beneficiaries' interests. Regular updates and communication with your estate planning attorney can further help in addressing these concerns effectively.

CHAPTER 20

MARRIED COUPLES WITHOUT CHILDREN

Estate Planning for Childless Couples and California Probate Code § 6402.5

For couples without children, estate planning can present unique challenges and opportunities. One significant aspect to consider is what happens to their estates upon their passing, especially under California law if they do not leave a will. California Probate Code § 6402.5 plays a crucial role in such situations, particularly affecting how estates are handled in the absence of a will (intestate succession). Understanding this law is essential for childless couples in California to ensure their assets are distributed according to their wishes.

Overview of California Probate Code § 6402.5

California Probate Code § 6402.5 specifies the distribution of assets when a married individual dies intestate (without a will) and is survived by a spouse but no children, parents, siblings, or nieces/nephews. The law is designed to address the scenario where assets might unfairly benefit only one side of the family in the absence of direct descendants.

- Application of § 6402.5: This section applies when a decedent's surviving spouse inherits community property and/or quasi-community property. If the decedent also has separate property, and there are no surviving children, parents, siblings, or descendants of deceased siblings, then one-half of the separate property is distributed to the surviving spouse, and the other half is distributed to the deceased spouse's next of kin in accordance with the regular rules of intestate succession.
- Purpose: The purpose of this statute is to ensure that the deceased spouse's family retains some interest in the estate, recognizing that both spouses may have contributed to their community from different sources throughout their marriage.

Issues and Considerations for Childless Couples

1. Risk of Partial Distribution to Extended Family: For childless couples, the application of § 6402.5 means that if one spouse dies without a will, a portion of their estate could automatically go to their relatives rather than entirely to the surviving spouse. This might not reflect the couple's mutual wishes, especially if they prefer that their entire estate ultimately benefit their spouse.
2. Estate Division Complications: Without clear estate planning, extended family members of the first spouse to die could inherit assets, potentially leading to disputes or complications, especially if the surviving spouse had different intentions.

Estate Planning Strategies

1. Creating a Will or Trust: The most straightforward way to avoid unintended consequences of intestate succession is for each spouse to have a will or trust that clearly states their wishes for the distribution of their assets.
2. Comprehensive Estate Plan: Couples should consider a comprehensive estate plan that includes wills, trusts, durable powers of attorney, and advance healthcare directives. This ensures that all aspects of their wishes are covered, from healthcare decisions to the distribution of their assets.
3. Regular Review and Updates: Estate plans should be reviewed and updated regularly, especially after significant life events or changes in the law, to ensure they still reflect the couple's wishes.
4. Spousal Property Petitions: In some cases, the surviving spouse might use a spousal property petition to simplify transferring assets after the first spouse's death. This can be an effective tool, but it's important to understand its limitations and ensure it fits within a broader estate planning strategy.

Conclusion

For childless couples in California, understanding and planning around Probate Code § 6402.5 is essential. Without proper planning, there is a risk that a significant portion of one spouse's estate could pass to relatives other than the surviving spouse. Effective estate planning, including the creation of wills and trusts, ensures that assets are distributed according to the couple's wishes, safeguarding their legacy and providing peace of mind.

CHAPTER 21

DISINHERITING A CHILD OR OTHER FAMILY MEMBER

Estate Planning Challenges of Disinheriting a Child

Disinheriting a child is a significant decision that comes with its own set of legal and emotional challenges. Whether due to estrangement, differences in values, or other personal reasons, the choice to disinherit a child should be carefully considered and properly executed to ensure that the estate plan reflects the parent's intentions without leading to unnecessary legal disputes. Here are the unique issues and strategies involved in effectively disinheriting a child.

Legal and Emotional Considerations

1. Legal Challenges: Disinherited children may feel aggrieved and seek to challenge the will or trust, claiming that it does not reflect the parent's true intentions. They might argue that the parent was unduly influenced by others or not of sound mind when making the decision. These lawsuits are especially messy because they involve family members suing each other.
2. Family Dynamics: The decision to disinherit a child can exacerbate existing family tensions and lead to long-term divisions among siblings and other relatives. It's important to consider the broader impact on family relationships.
3. State Laws: Each state has specific laws regarding disinheritance. Some states protect children under certain conditions, particularly minor children, from complete disinheritance to ensure their support and welfare.

Counseling Required to Properly Disinherit a Child

Disinheriting a child requires specific counseling from the estate planning attorney. Under California Probate Code §812, a testator must be able to communicate verbally, or by other means, the decision, and to understand and appreciate, to the extent relevant, the following:

- The rights, duties and responsibilities created by, or affected by the decision;
- The probable consequences for the decisionmaker and as appropriate, the persons affected by the decision; and
- The significant risks, benefits, and reasonable alternatives involved in the decision.

This requires that the estate planning attorney, as the witness to their wishes, properly counsel the client, so as to understand and appreciate, on the following:

1. Explain intestate succession
2. Explain that what they want is to change intestate succession
3. That the consequence of the disinheritance decision is twofold:

4. The disinherited person gets less
5. The other beneficiaries get more
6. Explain the possibility that the disinherited person may sue
7. Explain how the "no contest clause" works
8. Ask if the client understands and confirms the disinheritance decision

Strategies for Disinheriting a Child

1. Explicit Statements in Estate Documents: To avoid ambiguity and potential legal challenges, it's crucial to explicitly state in your will or trust that you intend to disinherit the child. Merely omitting the child's name from the document might not be sufficient as it could be perceived as an oversight. A clear statement clarifies that the omission is intentional.
2. Provide a Reason: While not legally necessary, providing a reason for disinheriting a child can help reinforce the parent's decision and may reduce the likelihood of successful legal challenges. It can also provide closure or understanding to the family as to why this decision was made.
3. Use of a No-Contest Clause: Including a no-contest clause (also known as an "in terrorem" clause) in your trust can discourage legal challenges. This clause can state that if an heir challenges the trust and loses, they will forfeit any other inheritance they might have received. However, the effectiveness and enforceability of no-contest clauses depends on the circumstances.
4. Consider Trusts: Setting up a trust rather than using a will can provide more control and discretion in how your assets are managed and distributed. Trusts can be structured to minimize the chances of successful legal challenges from disinherited children.
5. Gifts During Lifetime: In some cases, parents might choose to give gifts to the child during their lifetime instead of through the will. This can serve as a way to provide for the child without including them in the trust, potentially reducing conflict after the parent's death.

6. Consult an Estate Planning Attorney: Because disinheriting a child can lead to significant legal and familial challenges, it is advisable to work with an experienced estate planning attorney. They can help navigate the legal requirements and craft an estate plan that minimally exposes the estate to the risk of litigation.

Conclusion

Disinheriting a child is a decision that carries significant implications, both legally and emotionally. Careful planning, clear communication, and the use of specific legal tools are essential to effectively implement this decision while minimizing its impact on family harmony and reducing the potential for costly, emotional, and time-consuming litigation. By considering the emotional and familial outcomes as well as the legal aspects, parents can make more informed decisions that align with their intentions and the well-being of the family.

CHAPTER 22
PROTECTION OF AN ESTATE PLAN

Protection of an Estate Plan

Most folks think that their only option is to give an inheritance directly and outright to their beneficiaries. Often times, giving money directly to your beneficiaries can be a disaster. If you give the inheritance directly to your child and then that child gets a divorce, then your daughter-in-law or son-in-law would have an interest in that inheritance. If you give an inheritance directly to a beneficiary who has drug, alcohol, or gambling addictions, they're susceptible to spending their inheritance on things you probably wouldn't approve of. If you give an inheritance directly to someone who has poor money management skills, they may squander their inheritance.

These risks need to be planned for to ensure that your heir doesn't lose their inheritance and end up with nothing. An inheritance is like giving a big pile of cash to a beneficiary, similar to winning the lottery. You may want to add certain protections to prevent your beneficiary from losing all of their inheritance. To provide this protection, we can create a protective sub-trust where assets are held for the benefit of your heirs. This sub-trust will include spendthrift clauses, which will protect your loved ones from divorce, creditors, poor financial decisions, and external threats. The sub-trust can also provide protection if your loved ones are disabled or incapacitated, or if they receive government benefits, by shielding the assets from lawsuits, bankruptcy, and creditors.

Spendthrift Trust

A spendthrift trust is a trust that includes a spendthrift clause. A spendthrift clause prevents the trustee from giving any of the trust assets directly to the beneficiary's creditors. It protects the beneficiary from bankruptcy, lawsuits, divorce, and creditors, keeping the trust assets separate from the beneficiary's personal property. This protection is not something that an individual can create for themselves; California law does not allow a person to create a spendthrift trust to protect their own assets from creditors. However, you can create a spendthrift trust for your loved ones, allowing you to provide for their future while keeping their inheritance secure.

Special Needs Trust

A special needs trust is a protective sub-trust created for a beneficiary who has special needs. Special needs could include any disability that qualifies an individual for needs-based government benefits. To qualify for such benefits, an individual cannot have more than $2,000 of countable assets. Countable assets include investments, rental properties, brokerage or securities accounts, and cash. Needs-based government benefits may include Medicaid (Medi-Cal) for healthcare costs, Supplemental Security Income (SSI) from the Social Security Administration, or In-Home

Supportive Services (IHSS), which provides caregiver support for individuals with disabilities.

If you leave an inheritance directly to a beneficiary with special needs, they may become ineligible for these types of government benefits. To ensure they remain eligible, we can create a special needs sub-trust at your passing to provide ongoing support for a beneficiary with special needs while preserving their access to government benefits.

No-Contest Clause

Another protection we build into an estate plan is a no-contest clause. This clause discourages anyone from challenging the terms of your Revocable Living Trust by disinheriting them if they bring a contest lawsuit against it. The no-contest clause is designed to protect your wishes, ensuring that your decisions are respected and that the Successor Trustee follows your instructions.

Trust Protector

A trust protector is an important role that can further strengthen your estate plan. A trust protector is an independent third party appointed to oversee the trust and ensure it functions according to your wishes. The role of the trust protector may include modifying the terms of the trust if circumstances change, removing or replacing a trustee if necessary, and resolving disputes between the trustee and beneficiaries. This added layer of oversight ensures that the trust remains flexible and can adapt to changing laws or family circumstances.

For instance, if there are changes in tax laws or if family dynamics evolve, the trust protector has the authority to make necessary amendments to the trust to ensure it continues to meet your goals. The trust protector can also intervene if a trustee is not fulfilling their duties or if there are disagreements that could threaten the proper administration of the trust. By appointing a trust protector, you gain peace of mind knowing there is someone empowered to protect your interests and ensure your beneficiaries are cared for according to your intentions.

Summary

Adding protections to your estate plan helps secure the future of your beneficiaries, providing them with the resources they need while protecting their inheritance from external threats. By incorporating tools such as spendthrift trusts, special needs trusts, no-contest clauses, and appointing a trust protector, you can create a more resilient estate plan that safeguards your loved ones from potential risks. These measures ensure your wishes are honored, your beneficiaries are supported, and your assets are protected from mismanagement or threats, providing you with peace of mind and confidence in your estate plan.

CHAPTER 23

KEEPING YOUR PLAN UP TO DATE WITH YOUR CHANGING FAMILY DYNAMICS

The Importance of Keeping Your Estate Plan Up to Date

An estate plan is a vital tool that reflects your wishes for the distribution of your assets, the care of your loved ones, and your legacy after you pass. However, an estate plan is not a static document; it must evolve alongside your life circumstances, family dynamics, and legal changes. Failing to update an estate plan can lead to unintended consequences, legal complications, and potential disputes among family members. This section discusses the importance of keeping your estate plan up to date and regularly reviewing it to ensure it continues to meet your goals and reflect your current wishes.

Key Reasons to Keep Your Estate Plan Up to Date

1. Changes in Family Dynamics: Family relationships are dynamic and can shift over time. Whether due to marriages, divorces, births, deaths, or estrangement, these changes can dramatically affect your estate plan.

    - Marriage or Divorce: If you marry or divorce, failing to update your estate plan could result in your assets being distributed in a way that no longer aligns with your wishes. For instance, a former spouse may still be listed as a beneficiary or guardian.
    - Birth or Adoption of Children or Grandchildren: When a new child or grandchild enters the family, you'll want to ensure they are included in your estate plan. Similarly, changes in a child's needs (such as a special needs child or a child going through a tough financial situation) may require an update to your estate plan.
    - Death of a Beneficiary or Trustee: If a beneficiary or someone named as an executor, trustee, or guardian dies, it is essential to amend the plan to reflect new roles and distributions.
    - Estrangement or Reconciliation: Family relationships can change over time, and your plan should reflect whether you wish to disinherit someone or welcome someone back into the fold.

2. Shifts in Financial Circumstances: Changes in your financial situation, such as acquiring new property, starting or selling a business, or experiencing a significant increase or decrease in wealth, require revisiting your estate plan.

    - New Assets: If you acquire new significant assets (such as real estate or business interests), these should be included in your estate plan to ensure they are distributed according to your wishes.
    - Debt or Financial Hardships: If your financial situation changes for the worse, you may need to update your estate

plan to address outstanding debts or ensure that creditors do not claim too much of your estate.

3. Shifts in Personal Goals and Wishes: As your personal goals and priorities evolve, so too should your estate plan. For example, you may want to modify your estate to reflect new charitable interests or adjust how much you leave to certain family members.
4. Changes in Laws and Tax Codes: Estate planning laws and tax regulations can change over time. Changes in federal or state estate taxes, trust regulations, or inheritance laws may necessitate revisions to your plan to minimize tax liabilities or ensure compliance with new legal requirements.

    - Estate Tax Thresholds: If estate tax laws change and the threshold for taxable estates is adjusted, you may need to update your estate plan to reduce tax exposure.
    - Trust and Probate Laws: If laws governing trusts or probate procedures are updated, your plan might need to be adjusted to reflect the new legal landscape and ensure its enforceability.

5. Executor and Trustee Selection: The individuals you choose to serve as your executor, trustee, or guardian should be reviewed regularly. As relationships evolve and circumstances change, these roles may need to be reassigned to someone better suited or more available to fulfill these responsibilities.
6. Healthcare and Incapacity Directives: Documents like a healthcare directive or power of attorney need to be kept current to ensure that the individuals you trust to make decisions on your behalf are still the right choices. Regular updates ensure that these documents reflect your most current wishes, especially in situations involving changing medical conditions or advancing age.

The Risks of Not Updating Your Estate Plan

Failing to update your estate plan can lead to numerous unintended consequences, including:

- Unintended Beneficiaries: If you fail to update your plan, assets may pass to someone you no longer intend to benefit, such as an ex-spouse or estranged family member.
- Family Disputes: Outdated plans can result in confusion or disputes among heirs, particularly if family dynamics have changed but your estate plan has not kept pace.
- Increased Taxes and Legal Fees: Without an up-to-date estate plan, your estate may be subject to avoidable taxes or legal fees. This can reduce the amount that ultimately passes to your intended beneficiaries.
- Inadequate Provisions for Dependents: If your family has grown or your dependents' needs have changed, failing to revise your estate plan may leave them inadequately provided for.

Regularly Reviewing Your Estate Plan

Experts recommend reviewing your estate plan every three to five years or after significant life events, such as:

- Marriage or divorce
- Birth or adoption of children or grandchildren
- Major changes in financial circumstances
- Purchase or sale of significant assets (business, real estate, etc.)
- Death or incapacitation of a beneficiary, trustee, or executor
- Changes in tax laws or estate planning laws

Regular reviews ensure that your plan reflects your most current circumstances, goals, and wishes.

Conclusion

Keeping your estate plan up to date is crucial for ensuring that your legacy is distributed according to your wishes and that your family is protected. By regularly reviewing and updating your plan to reflect changes in family dynamics, financial situations, personal goals, and legal requirements, you can avoid potential disputes, reduce tax liabilities, and provide peace of mind to you and your loved ones. An experienced estate planning attorney can help guide you through this process and make the necessary adjustments to keep your estate plan current and effective.

CHAPTER 24

KEEPING YOUR ASSETS ALIGNED WITH YOUR ESTATE PLAN

Ensuring Your Assets Are Aligned with Your Estate Plan

A well-drafted estate plan is the foundation for ensuring your wishes are carried out after your death, but it is only as effective as the alignment of your assets with that plan. One of the most common mistakes in estate planning is failing to properly title or align assets with the estate plan's structures, especially with a trust. This oversight can result in assets bypassing the intended estate plan, causing unintended distributions, probate delays, and potential legal conflicts.

Here, we explore why it's crucial to keep your assets aligned with your estate plan, focusing on cash bank accounts, brokerage accounts, real estate, retirement accounts, life insurance, and annuities. Regularly reviewing and updating the titling of your assets and beneficiary designations is essential to ensure your estate plan works as intended.

Trusts and Asset Titling

A common estate planning tool is a revocable living trust, which is designed to avoid probate, protect your privacy, and manage your assets both during your life and after your death. However, for a trust to effectively control your assets, those assets must be titled in the name of the trust. This is a critical step that is often overlooked.

- Cash Bank Accounts: Bank accounts such as checking, savings, and certificates of deposit (CDs) should be retitled in the name of your trust. If these accounts remain in your name and are not transferred to the trust, they will likely have to go through probate, defeating one of the primary advantages of having a trust.
- Brokerage Accounts: Similarly, your investment and brokerage accounts should be retitled in the name of your trust. If these accounts are not transferred into the trust, they may be subject to probate, and their distribution may not follow the guidelines set out in your trust.
- Real Estate: One of the most valuable assets many people own is real estate. For your trust to control your real estate holdings (whether it's your primary residence or investment properties), the deeds to your properties must be retitled in the name of the trust. If the title remains in your name, your property may not pass to your intended beneficiaries without going through the probate process, which can be time-consuming and costly.

Consequences of Failing to Retitle Assets

If assets such as bank accounts, brokerage accounts, or real estate are not properly titled in the name of the trust, they will not be governed by the trust's terms. Instead, they may go through probate and be distributed according to California law or a will (if one exists). This can create delays, added expenses, and unintended distributions.

Beneficiary Designations: Retirement Accounts, Life Insurance, and Annuities

In contrast to cash and real estate, retirement accounts (like IRAs, 401(k)s), life insurance policies, and annuities are not controlled by a trust in the same way. These assets pass directly to the beneficiaries named in the policy or account, bypassing probate. Therefore, it is critical that these accounts have properly named beneficiaries to ensure they are distributed as intended.

- Retirement Accounts: Your retirement accounts should have up-to-date beneficiary designations that reflect your current wishes. Failing to name a beneficiary (or naming an outdated or deceased beneficiary) can cause significant tax implications and delays in distribution. In some cases, the retirement account could be forced into probate, subjecting it to more taxation and complications.
- Life Insurance Policies: Like retirement accounts, life insurance proceeds are paid directly to the named beneficiaries. It's important to ensure that your beneficiary designations reflect your current circumstances. If no beneficiary is named, the proceeds could become part of your probate estate, which may reduce the benefits due to administrative fees and taxes.
- Annuities: Annuities also rely on beneficiary designations to determine who receives the payout after your death. Without a current and accurate beneficiary designation, the annuity could pass through probate, needlessly costing time and money.

Monitoring and Maintaining Asset Alignment

Even if you've initially titled your assets correctly and named the appropriate beneficiaries, ongoing monitoring is essential. Life circumstances change, and your estate plan needs to evolve accordingly. Regularly review your accounts and documents to ensure that everything remains properly aligned with your estate plan.

Key Steps to Keep Assets Aligned:

1. Review Asset Titling: Periodically check that all bank accounts, brokerage accounts, and real estate properties are still titled in the name of your trust. This is especially important if you've recently acquired new assets or sold old ones.
2. Update Beneficiary Designations: Life changes, such as the birth of children, marriage, divorce, or the death of a named beneficiary, should prompt a review and update of your beneficiary designations on retirement accounts, life insurance policies, and annuities.
3. Coordinate with an Attorney: Regularly meet with your estate planning attorney to review your estate plan and ensure that all new assets are properly titled or designated in accordance with your plan. They can also help navigate any changes in tax laws or regulations that might impact your estate.
4. Track Major Life Changes: Any significant life event—such as marriage, the birth of a child or grandchild, divorce, or the death of a loved one—should trigger a review of your estate plan. Make sure your estate reflects your new family dynamics and that your assets are protected and distributed according to your current wishes.

Conclusion

An estate plan is only effective when your assets are properly aligned with its directives. Titling bank accounts, brokerage accounts, and real estate in the name of your trust and keeping beneficiary designations on retirement accounts, life insurance, and annuities up to date are critical steps to ensuring that your assets are distributed according to your wishes. By regularly reviewing and adjusting asset alignment, you can avoid probate, protect your wealth, and provide for your loved ones as intended.

CHAPTER 25
CALIFORNIA PROPERTY TAX ISSUES WITH YOUR ESTATE PLAN

California Property Tax Issues

Property taxes are a significant consideration in estate planning, particularly for California homeowners looking to preserve the value of their property for their heirs. California has a long history of property tax laws designed to limit tax increases, most notably through Proposition 13. However, Proposition 19, passed in 2020, has introduced new restrictions and requirements that directly impact how homeowners can transfer their property tax base to children or grandchildren.

This chapter will focus on how Proposition 19 affects property tax transfers of family homes, particularly the conditions required to maintain a lower property tax base under Proposition 13. We will also explore the requirements both the transferor (the person transferring the property) and the transferee (the person receiving the property) must meet, along with the additional steps to avoid a property tax reassessment that could lead to higher taxes.

Proposition 13: The Original Property Tax Protection

To understand Proposition 19, it's essential first to grasp the protections of Proposition 13, passed in 1978. Proposition 13 caps property tax increases by limiting the annual increase of assessed property value to 2%, regardless of how much the market value rises. This allows property owners to enjoy relatively low property taxes compared to the rising value of their homes over time.

Previously Proposition 58 and Proposition 193 allowed property owners to pass on this low property tax base to their children or grandchildren. Prior to Proposition 19, homeowners could transfer the primary residence and a limited amount of other properties to their heirs without reassessment, meaning that the property taxes would not rise to current market rates, preserving the original low tax base.

Proposition 19: Key Changes to Property Tax Transfers

Proposition 19, passed in November 2020 and effective in February 2021, introduced significant changes to property tax transfers between parents (or grandparents) and children (or grandchildren). It narrowed the conditions under which a property could be transferred without reassessment, and thus without a significant increase in property taxes.

The key changes under Proposition 19 include:

1. Primary Residence Restriction: Proposition 19 only allows the transfer of the low property tax base for a primary residence. Transfers of second homes, vacation homes, or investment

properties to heirs will trigger a reassessment of the property at current market value, leading to higher property taxes.

2. New Residency Requirements: Both the transferor (the person transferring the property) and the transferee (the person receiving the property) must use the property as their primary residence, as determined by filing for a homeowner's exemption or disabled veteran's exemption, for the lower property tax base to be transferred. This new rule imposes significant restrictions on how and when the property can be transferred to avoid reassessment.
3. Limitation on Equity Transferred: Prop 19 puts a cap of one million dollars ($1,000,000) on the amount of equity that can be transferred in the primary residence before it is reassessed for property tax purposes. That means that if the difference between the assessed value and the current fair market value is more than one million dollars, then the excess over one million dollars will be reassessed for property tax purposes.

Requirements to Avoid Reassessment under Proposition 19

To avoid a property tax reassessment under Proposition 19 and retain the Proposition 13 tax base, the following conditions must be met:

1. Primary Residence of the Transferor: The property must have been the primary residence of the parent or grandparent transferring the property at the time of the transfer. This means the property must be where the transferor was living and claiming their homeowner's exemption or disabled veteran's exemption, which provides a property tax reduction for the primary residence.
2. Primary Residence of the Transferee: The child or grandchild receiving the property must also make the home their primary residence within a year of the transfer. This is a critical change from the previous law, where the transferee did not need to live in the property for the lower tax base to apply. The transferee must claim the homeowner's exemption or disabled veteran's

exemption with the county assessor's office to demonstrate that the property is their primary residence.

3. Filing a Homeowners Exemption: Both the transferor and transferee must file a homeowner's exemption or disabled veteran's exemption with the county assessor's office. This exemption not only shows that the property is being used as the primary residence, but it also helps verify compliance with the requirements of Proposition 19.
4. Value Limitations: Under Proposition 19, there is a cap on the value of the property that can be transferred without reassessment. The low tax base can be transferred only if the current market value of the home is within $1 million of the original assessed value. If the market value exceeds this limit, the property will be partially reassessed, resulting in a higher property tax bill, though it will still be lower than if the full reassessment occurred.

Example Scenario of Proposition 19 Application

Let's consider a typical example to illustrate how Proposition 19 applies:

Parents' Residence: A couple has owned their home for 20 years, with an assessed value of $300,000. Due to Proposition 13, they pay property taxes based on that value, even though the market value of the home is now $1.5 million.

Passing to Their Child: Upon their death, the home is left to their child. Under Proposition 19, if the child wants to keep the home and retain the low property tax base, they must move into the house and claim it as their primary residence within one year.

Homeowners Exemption: The child files the necessary homeowner's exemption with the county assessor, confirming that the home is their primary residence.

Value Cap: Since the current market value ($1.5 million) exceeds the assessed value by more than $1 million, there will be a partial reassessment. The new taxable value will be based on the $1 million cap, resulting in a higher tax bill than the parents had but still lower than a full reassessment to market value.

If the child chooses not to live in the home, the property will be fully reassessed to its current market value of $1.5 million, and property taxes will increase accordingly.

Pros and Cons of Proposition 19

Pros:

- Preventing Abuse of Property Tax Protections: Proposition 19 ensures that property tax protections are used for family homes and not for transferring vacation homes or investment properties to the next generation without tax consequences.
- Limited Transfer of Tax Benefits: It preserves the ability to transfer property tax benefits for families who want to keep their home within the family.
- Flexibility for Seniors and Disaster Victims: Proposition 19 also allows seniors, disabled homeowners, and wildfire/disaster victims to transfer their property tax base to a new home, providing flexibility if they need to move.

Cons:

- Residency Requirement: The requirement for the child or grandchild to live in the home as their primary residence is a significant limitation, particularly if the family member cannot or does not want to live in the inherited property.
- Partial Reassessments: If the property's market value exceeds the $1 million cap, heirs may still face higher property taxes, which can make it difficult to maintain ownership of the family home.
- Increased Complexity: The new rules add complexity to estate planning, requiring families to carefully plan and coordinate around these new restrictions.

Conclusion

Proposition 19 introduced significant changes to California's property tax laws that impact how parents and grandparents can transfer property to their children or grandchildren. The key to preserving the low property tax base under Proposition 13 is for both the transferor and transferee to use the home as their primary residence and to file the appropriate homeowner's exemptions with the county assessor. Regular review of your estate plan and property ownership structure is essential to ensure that your heirs can benefit from the available property tax protections while avoiding unexpected tax burdens or reassessments.

Working closely with an estate planning attorney and understanding the intricacies of Proposition 19 can help you preserve your family home and manage property tax implications effectively for future generations.

CHAPTER 26

SAVING ON CAPITAL GAINS TAXES

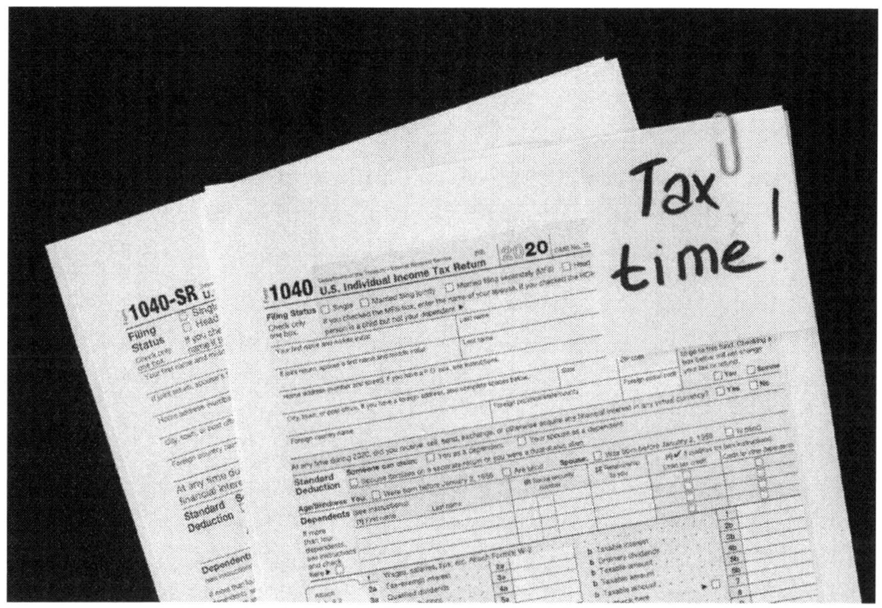

Impact of the Step-Up in Basis Rules on an Estate Plan

One of the most valuable tax benefits available upon the death of a property owner is the step-up in basis rule. This rule affects the basis of inherited property for capital gains tax purposes, which can significantly impact an estate plan. Understanding how the step-up in basis works, especially for married couples, and structuring property ownership accordingly is essential for minimizing tax burdens on heirs.

What Is a Step-Up in Basis?

Basis refers to the original purchase price of an asset, adjusted for improvements, depreciation, or other factors. When you sell an asset, such as real estate, the capital gains tax is calculated on the difference between the sale price and the basis. For example, if you purchased a home for $200,000 and sold it for $500,000, your capital gain would be $300,000, which would be subject to capital gains tax.

However, upon the death of the property owner, the step-up in basis rule allows the property's basis to be adjusted (or "stepped up") to its fair market value at the time of the owner's death. This means that when heirs inherit the property and eventually sell it, the capital gains tax will be calculated based on the stepped-up value, which can substantially reduce or eliminate the capital gains tax. This could significantly reduce capital gains tax.

Example:

If a parent purchased a home for $200,000 and it was worth $1,000,000 at the time of their death, the property's basis would "step up" to $1,000,000. If the heirs later sell the property for $1,050,000, they will only pay capital gains tax on the $50,000 gain, rather than the $850,000 gain that would have occurred if the original $200,000 basis had been used.

This step-up in basis is one of the reasons why real estate is often a favorable asset to inherit, as it allows heirs to minimize or eliminate capital gains taxes.

Step-Up in Basis for Married Couples

For married couples, the step-up in basis rules can become even more favorable, depending on how the property is titled. The way in which the property is held can significantly affect the capital gains tax burden when the second spouse passes away.

Community Property vs. Joint Tenancy

In California, a community property state, married couples have the option to hold property in different forms, such as joint tenancy or community property with right of survivorship. The form of ownership affects whether the surviving spouse receives a partial or full step-up in basis upon the first spouse's death.

1. Joint Tenancy: When a married couple holds property as joint tenants, only the deceased spouse's share of the property receives a step-up in basis. The surviving spouse's share retains the original basis.

Example for Married Couple Joint Tenancy: If a married couple holds property worth $1,000,000 as joint tenants, and their original purchase price was $200,000, only half of the property's value would receive a step-up in basis when one spouse dies. The deceased spouse's half would be stepped up to $500,000 (half of the $1,000,000 value), while the surviving spouse's half retains the original basis of $100,000. This means that upon sale, the surviving spouse's total basis in the property is $600,000 and could face significant capital gains tax when selling the property.

2. Community Property: In contrast, when the property is titled as community property (or community property with right of survivorship), both halves of the property receive a step-up in basis upon the death of the first spouse, regardless of which spouse originally contributed to the purchase of the property.

Example for Married Couple Community Property: If a married couple holds property worth $1,000,000 as community property and their original purchase price was $200,000, the entire property receives a step-up in basis to $1,000,000 upon the death of the first spouse. If the surviving spouse later sells the property for $1,000,000, there is no gain on the sale and therefore no capital gains tax due to the full step-up in basis of the community property.

Why the Step-Up in Basis Matters

The full step-up in basis available with community property can result in significant tax savings for the surviving spouse and heirs. With joint tenancy, the surviving spouse could face a substantial capital gains tax liability if they sell the property, as only half of the property receives the step-up. With community property, both halves receive the step-up, meaning much less or no capital gains tax will be owed if the property is sold shortly after the first spouse's death.

Fixing Property Ownership: Changing from Joint Tenancy to Community Property

Many married couples don't seek legal advice and inadvertently take title to their home as joint tenants rather than community property. This is often due to the common practice of titling property as "husband and wife, as joint tenants." Fortunately, couples can correct this and take advantage of the full step-up in basis by changing the way their property is titled to "husband and wife, as community property with the right of survivorship."

How to Change Property Title to Community Property with Right of Survivorship

1. Transferring Title: A married couple can transfer their jointly held property into "husband and wife as community property with right of survivorship" by executing a new deed. This is a straightforward process but requires care to ensure the new title is correctly recorded with the county assessor.
2. Recording a New Deed: The couple would need to record a new deed with the county, changing the vesting from "husband and wife, as joint tenants" to "husband and wife, as community property with right of survivorship." This ensures that both spouses' shares of the property will receive the step-up in basis upon the death of the first spouse.

Benefits of Changing Title

- Full Step-Up in Basis: Changing the title to community property with right of survivorship ensures that the entire property receives the step-up in basis, reducing capital gains tax liability for the surviving spouse and potentially for heirs.
- Retaining Survivorship Rights: By using "community property with right of survivorship," the surviving spouse automatically inherits the property upon the first spouse's death, avoiding the need for probate while still benefiting from the full step-up in basis.

Important Considerations

- Consider Property Taxes: Recording a deed involves a transfer of title that may allow the county assessor to reassess the property for property tax purposes. You will need to file the right documents, filled out correctly, with the assessor's office to exclude the house from reassessment for property tax purposes.
- Consult with an Attorney: Although the process of changing title is simple, it's important to consult with an estate planning attorney or real estate attorney to ensure that the transfer is done properly, and that all documentation is correctly filed.
- Retitling Other Assets: In addition to real estate, couples should consider whether other assets, such as brokerage accounts, should also be retitled to benefit from the full step-up in basis.

Conclusion

Understanding and leveraging the step-up in basis rules is a powerful tool in estate planning, especially for real estate and other valuable assets. For married couples, holding property as community property with right of survivorship offers the benefit of a full step-up in basis upon the death of the first spouse, which can dramatically reduce capital gains taxes when the property is eventually sold. Couples who have taken title as joint tenants can easily remedy this by transferring the property into community property, ensuring they take full advantage of the tax benefits available to them and safeguarding their assets for future generations.

By regularly reviewing the titling of assets and considering the impact of the step-up in basis, you can ensure that your estate plan provides the maximum tax benefits for your heirs.

CHAPTER 27

WHAT IS YOUR LAW FIRM 'S APPROACH TOWARDS CLIENTS?

Our Approach Towards Clients

We believe that there is nothing more important than family. We believe in protecting our family, teaching family history, values, traditions, culture, memories, and even favorite meal recipes. We believe in leaving a lasting legacy for our family.

To accomplish this, we believe that part of taking care of your family is to plan for the future and have a written plan of action to give a roadmap to safely navigate in times of crisis without panic or a fight breaking out.

We help our clients create an estate plan with integrity, professionalism, and education to ensure they understand what they have and what it does. Some clients who come to us with an existing estate plan learn new things that their previous attorney didn't explain to them. We aim to guide clients and provide the knowledge they need to make informed decisions about their future.

Our approach to estate planning is not just to have a client come in once, draft their estate plan, and never see them again. We want to have an ongoing relationship with our clients to make sure that the estate plan we design, and build is properly managed, maintained, and updated as needed.

Many estate plans fail because they are not reviewed regularly. We recommend that clients review their estate plan annually when they do their taxes. This review doesn't necessarily require an office visit but should involve checking to ensure that all assets are properly aligned and determining if any changes need to be made.

We also encourage clients to visit us at least every three years for a free consultation. During these check-ins, we review whether there have been any changes in tax laws, family dynamics, or assets that require updates to the estate plan.

How Often and Why Do You Recommend an Estate Plan Checkup?

There are certain times when someone needs to update their estate plan, such as when new legislation changes the best approach or when there are significant life changes. This includes events like marriage, divorce, death, or the addition of a new family member. We encourage clients to come in and speak with us at least every three years for a free consultation.

We provide notices to clients about any changes in tax laws or other legal updates, and we offer a free checkup meeting every three years to help keep their estate plans current. Additionally, we offer a free meeting for their trustee in the event of a client's disability or death. We also provide free phone calls to answer questions about the estate planning documents we have already created for them.

What is Asset Alignment and How Does It Play Into an Estate Plan?

Asset alignment involves ensuring that all of your assets are transferred according to your wishes upon your passing. The number one asset we need to ensure is properly placed in a trust is your home, along with any rental or investment real estate, including timeshares and vacant land. Real estate is often the first asset that can trigger probate, so aligning these assets with your estate plan helps to avoid that process. We also need to make sure financial accounts are titled in the trust or have designated beneficiaries.

Clients sometimes go to a new bank and open an account without adding it to the trust. Similarly, if a client buys a new home and sells the old one, they may forget to transfer the new property into the trust. If the home is refinanced, some lenders require it to be taken out of the trust temporarily, but it must be transferred back in afterward. This is why regular meetings with clients are essential—to ensure that their assets are properly aligned with their estate plan and their intentions.

CHAPTER 28
THE VALUE OF HIRING AN EXPERIENCED ATTORNEY

The Value of Hiring an Experienced Estate Planning Attorney

We want to make sure that an estate plan is done right the first time because if something wasn't done correctly, it may be too late once the error is discovered. Our office provides ongoing support to clients for education, to answer any questions they have, and for ongoing maintenance and support. We offer professional advice and education so clients understand their options and can make the right choices for them.

Certainly, the biggest value to any of our clients is peace of mind. They want the peace of mind of knowing that they are taken care of and that their loved ones are provided for.

What sets our firm apart in handling estate plans for our clients is that we offer professional counseling. We provide education so that clients understand their options and how best to choose based on their situation. We provide a process and a framework for clients to create an estate plan, and we're always there for them when they need us.

The Dangers of Today's Do-It-Yourself Trends in Estate Planning

We understand the desire to save money by seeking cheaper alternatives to an experienced estate planning attorney. Some people may even attempt to create their own estate plan with forms they find on the internet. However, let me caution you that being cheap can be expensive. Here are some major pitfalls that many families fall into.

The first pitfall is using forms found online or buying prepackaged software with templates for estate planning documents. You might save money by attempting this yourself, but without the necessary expertise, you are more likely to make mistakes.

Estate planning is not as simple as it seems. You may create a trust but may not fully understand what it provides. Then, you might not complete the second step of funding the trust properly, which means your trust won't avoid probate. The worst part is that you won't know you've made a mistake until it's too late.

You wouldn't perform your own surgery, and creating an estate plan with assets that you have spent a lifetime accumulating should not be treated as a do-it-yourself project. You need a seasoned professional to help you design and draft your estate plan and keep it up to date.

The second common mistake is going to a bargain attorney or a paralegal. Often, a bargain attorney or paralegal does not specialize solely in estate planning. They may also practice bankruptcy, family law, criminal law, or employment law. Because they lack specialized expertise in estate planning, you may not receive the level of support and guidance you need. Paralegals cannot provide legal advice, and the danger is that they may not fully understand the pitfalls and complexities of estate planning. Ultimately, you get what you pay for.

I once had a client who went to a paralegal to draft an estate plan because her husband had terminal cancer. The Revocable Living Trust that was drafted contained provisions the client didn't understand and did not want to keep, but because the trust became irrevocable upon her husband's death, she needed a court procedure to fix it. Additionally, the paralegal failed to correctly transfer the home, resulting in the need for another court procedure to fix the deed. The client ended up paying much more in legal fees to fix these mistakes than it would have cost to have an estate planning attorney do it right the first time.

The third pitfall is assuming that all estate plans or trusts are the same. Estate plans and trusts are not one-size-fits-all. Your estate plan must be custom-designed and drafted to fit your particular situation. You need the right documents, backed by an ongoing relationship with your estate planning attorney to keep the plan up to date. Assuming that all estate plans or attorneys are the same can be a costly mistake.

GLOSSARY OF COMMON ESTATE PLANNING TERMS

Advance Healthcare Directive: A document that appoints your healthcare agent and spells out your healthcare wishes if you become unable to communicate, such as what kind of medical treatment you do or do not want.

Assets: Everything owned by a person, including money, real estate, and personal belongings.

Asset Protection Trust: A trust designed to protect a person's assets from creditors, lawsuits, or other claims. It helps ensure that assets are preserved for the beneficiaries.

Bequeath: The legal term used to leave someone personal property in a will,

Bequest: The legal term used to describe personal property left in a will.

Blended Family: A family where one or both spouses have children from previous relationships. Estate planning for blended families often involves addressing the needs of both biological and stepchildren.

Beneficiary: A person or organization that receives assets, such as money or property, from a will, trust, life insurance policy, or retirement account after someone passes away.

Beneficiary Designation: The person you name to receive assets from specific accounts, such as a retirement account or life insurance policy, after your death.

Bloodline: The direct descendants of an individual, such as children, grandchildren, and further generations. Estate planning often focuses on preserving assets within the bloodline.

Bypass Trust (or Credit Shelter Trust): A trust used to

minimize estate taxes by taking advantage of the deceased spouse's estate tax exemption. It allows assets to pass to beneficiaries without being taxed when the surviving spouse dies.

Charitable Gift: A donation left to a charity or nonprofit organization, either during your lifetime or as part of your estate plan.

Codicil: An amendment to a will that makes changes, additions, or deletions without having to rewrite the entire will.

Community Property: A type of property ownership for married couples in some states, where both spouses equally own any property acquired during the marriage.

Deed: A written legal document that describes a piece of property and outlines its boundaries. The seller of a property transfers ownership by delivering the deed to the buyer in exchange for an agreed upon sum of money.

Devise: A legal term that now means any real or personal property that is transferred under the terms of a will. Previously, the term only referred to real property.

Disinherit: The act of intentionally leaving someone out of your will so that they do not receive any part of your estate.

Estate: Everything a person owns at the time of their death, including real estate, money, investments, and personal belongings.

Estate Tax: A tax on the value of a person's estate after they die. The amount of tax depends on the size of the estate and current tax laws.

Executor: The person named in a will who is responsible for managing and settling the deceased person's estate, including distributing assets and paying off debts.

Fair Market Value: That price for which an item of property would be purchased by a willing buyer, and sold by a willing seller, both knowing all the facts and neither being under any compulsion to buy or sell.

Fiduciary: A person who has the responsibility to manage someone else's money or property with care and loyalty.

Fiduciary Duty: An obligation to act in the best interest of another party. For instance, a corporation's board member has a fiduciary duty to the shareholders, a trustee has a fiduciary duty to the trust's beneficiaries, and an attorney has a fiduciary duty to a client.

Grantor (or Settlor): The person who creates a trust and transfers their assets into it.

Guardian: A person legally appointed to manage the personal and/or financial affairs of a minor or incapacitated person.

Guardianship: The legal responsibility for the care of a minor child or an incapacitated adult. A guardian can be named in a will to take care of dependents if both parents pass away.

Heir (Heir at Law): A person legally entitled to inherit property from the decedent if there is no will.

Holographic Will: A will that is handwritten and signed by the person making it, without witnesses.

Intestate: When someone dies without a will, they are said to have died intestate. In this case, the state's laws decide who will inherit their assets.

Irrevocable Trust: A trust that cannot be changed or revoked once it is created, usually used to help reduce taxes or protect assets.

Issue: The lineal descendants (biological children, adopted children, grandchildren, great-grandchildren etc.) of a person.

Joint Tenancy: A way for two or more people to own property together. When one owner dies, the property automatically goes to the surviving owner(s).

Living Trust: A type of trust that you create during your lifetime to manage your assets and decide who will inherit them after you die, often avoiding probate.

Minor: A person that is under the age of 18 years old. The term does not apply to an emancipated youth.

Next of Kin: The closest living relatives of the decedent.

No-Contest Clause: A clause in a will or trust that discourages beneficiaries from challenging the document in court. If they do challenge it, they risk losing their inheritance.

Personal Property: Items of tangible or intangible property that are not real estate or attached to the land.

Pour Over Will: A will that gives some or all assets of the decedent to a trust.

Power of Attorney: A legal document that gives someone else the authority to make decisions on your behalf if you become unable to do so. This can be for financial or medical matters.

Probate: The legal process of proving that a will is valid, paying debts, and distributing assets to beneficiaries. Probate can take time and may be costly and public.

Qualified Terminable Interest Property (QTIP) Trust: A trust that allows a surviving spouse to receive income from the trust for life, while the remainder of the assets go to other beneficiaries after the surviving spouse dies.

Real Property: Real estate or anything attached to the land, such as a building or house.

Residue: The remaining assets of the estate after all debts, taxes, and specific bequests have been paid.

Revocable Trust: A trust that can be changed or canceled by the person who created it (the grantor) during their lifetime. It becomes permanent after their death.

Self-Proving Will: A will is self-proving when it has certain language signed under penalty of perjury by the witnesses.

Specific Gift: A particular item or amount of money left to a beneficiary in a will, such as a specific piece of jewelry or a set amount of cash.

Spendthrift Trust: A trust set up to protect a beneficiary who might have trouble managing money. The trustee controls the funds, and the beneficiary cannot access all the money at once.

Statute: Any written law passed by a state or federal legislative body.

Step-Up in Basis: When property is inherited, its value is "stepped up" to the current market value at the time of the original owner's death. This can help reduce capital gains taxes if the property is sold.

Successor Trustee: A person or institution named to manage a trust after the original trustee dies or becomes unable to act.

Testate: When someone dies leaving a legal will.

Testator: The person who creates a will and decides how their assets will be distributed after their death.

Title: Ownership of property.

Trust: A legal arrangement where a person (called a trustee) manages assets for the benefit of others (called beneficiaries). Trusts can help avoid probate and reduce taxes.

Trust Amendment: A legal change made to an existing revocable trust to modify its terms without having to create a new trust.

Trustee: The person or entity (like a bank or law firm) responsible for managing and distributing assets held in a trust according to the terms set by the grantor.

Uniform Transfer to Minors Act: California law, which

provides a way for someone to give or leave property to a minor by appointing a "custodian" to manage the property for the minor.

Vesting: Expression of the form of legal title by which property is held, usually in a deed. An example of a vesting is "husband and wife, as joint tenants."

Will: A legal document that states how a person wants their assets to be distributed after they die. It can also include instructions for caring for minor children.

Will Contest: A proceeding peculiar to probate for the determination of questions of construction of a will or whether there is or is not a will. Any kind of litigated controversy concerning the eligibility of an instrument to probate as distinguished from validity of the contents of the will. (Will contests are in rem proceedings in that the contest is brought against the thing, the will, as opposed to in personam proceedings, which are brought against a person.)

Witness: A person who observes the signing of a will and attests to its authenticity.

Made in the USA
Middletown, DE
26 November 2024